BARNSLEY IN 50 BUILDINGS

KEIRON DUNN
WITH ILLUSTRATIONS BY JOHN HIGGINS

AMBERLEY

Dedicated to family and friends, especially those dearly departed.

First published 2023

Amberley Publishing, The Hill, Stroud
Gloucestershire GL5 4EP

www.amberley-books.com

British Library Cataloguing in Publication Data.
A catalogue record for this book is available from the British Library.

ISBN 978 1 3981 0034 3 (print)
ISBN 978 1 3981 0035 0 (ebook)

Typesetting by SJmagic DESIGN SERVICES, India.
Printed in Great Britain.

Contents

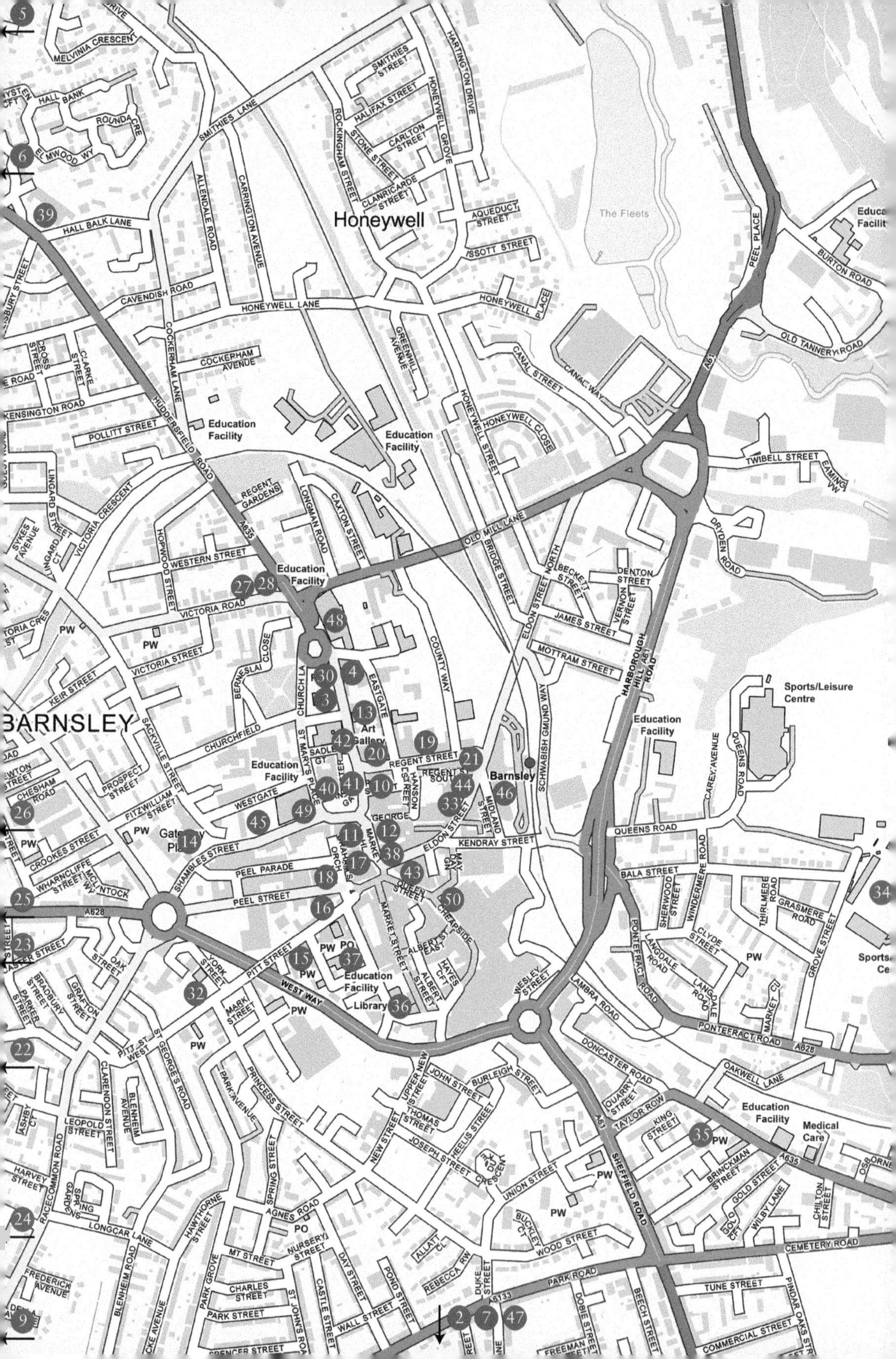

Honeywell
BARNSLEY
The Fleets
Barnsley
Education Facility
Art Gallery
Library
Gateway Plaza
Sports/Leisure Centre
Medical Care
PW
PO
MELVINIA CRESCENT
HALL BANK
ROUNDA CRE
ELMWOOD WY
HALL BALK LANE
SMITHIES LANE
SMITHIES STREET
HALIFAX STREET
STONE STREET
CARLTON STREET
CLANRICARDE STREET
ROCKINGHAM STREET
HONEYWELL GROVE
HARTINGTON DRIVE
AQUEDUCT STREET
ISSOTT STREET
ALLENDALE ROAD
CARRINGTON AVENUE
CAVENDISH ROAD
HONEYWELL LANE
HONEYWELL PLACE
GREENHILL AVENUE
CROSS STREET
CLARKE STREET
KENSINGTON ROAD
COCKERHAM LANE
COCKERHAM AVENUE
POLLITT STREET
HUDDERSFIELD ROAD
A635
CANAL STREET
CANAL WAY
HONEYWELL CLOSE
HONEYWELL STREET
PEEL PLACE
BURTON ROAD
OLD TANNERY ROAD
A61
TWIBELL STREET
EAMING WY
LINGARD STREET
VICTORIA CRESCENT
SYKES AVENUE
LINGARD CT
REGENT GARDENS
LONGMAN ROAD
CAXTON STREET
OLD MILL LANE
BRIDGE STREET
ELDON STREET NORTH
BECKETT STREET
DENTON STREET
VERNON STREET
JAMES STREET
DRYDEN ROAD
HOPWOOD STREET
WESTERN STREET
VICTORIA ROAD
MOTTRAM STREET
HARBOROUGH HILL ROAD
COUNTY WAY
VICTORIA STREET
BERNESLAI CLOSE
CHURCH LA
EASTGATE
KEIR STREET
SACKVILLE STREET
CHURCHFIELD
REGENT STREET
REGENT ST SOUTH
HANSON STREET
SCHWABISH GMUND WAY
CAREY AVENUE
QUEENS ROAD
ST MARY'S PLACE
SADLER GT
PROSPECT STREET
NEWTON STREET
CHESHAM ROAD
FITZWILLIAM STREET
WESTGATE
MIDLAND STREET
ELDON STREET
KENDRAY STREET
BALA STREET
SHERWOOD STREET
WINDERMERE ROAD
THIRLMERE ROAD
GRASMERE ROAD
CROOKES STREET
WHARNCLIFFE STREET
MCLINTOCK WY
SHAMBLES STREET
PEEL PARADE
PEEL STREET
MARKET HILL
QUEEN STREET
CHEAPSIDE
MAY DAY GN
A628
PONTEFRACT ROAD
LANGDALE ROAD
CLYDE STREET
GROVE STREET
YORK STREET
OAK STREET
PITT STREET
WEST WAY
MARKET STREET
ALBERT ST EAST
ALBERT STREET
HAYES CFT
WESLEY STREET
LAMBRA ROAD
MARKET CL
BRADBURY STREET
PARKER STREET
GRAFTON STREET
MARK STREET
PITT ST WEST
ST GEORGE'S ROAD
DONCASTER ROAD
OAKWELL LANE
UPPER NEW STREET
JOHN STREET
BURLEIGH STREET
PARK AVENUE
PRINCESS STREET
CLARENDON STREET
BLENHEIM AVENUE
LEOPOLD STREET
ASHBY CT
THOMAS STREET
HEELIS STREET
JOSEPH STREET
NEW STREET
DUKE CRESCENT
QUARRY STREET
TAYLOR ROW
KING STREET
BRINCKMAN STREET
GOLD STREET
GOLD CFT
WILBY LANE
CHILTON STREET
HARVEY STREET
RACECOMMON ROAD
SPRING GARDENS
SPRING STREET
AGNES ROAD
UNION STREET
BUCKLEY CT
WOOD STREET
SHEFFIELD ROAD
CEMETERY ROAD
LONGCAR LANE
HAWTHORNE STREET
NURSERY STREET
ALLATT CL
REBECCA RW
DUKE STREET
A6133
PARK ROAD
FREDERICK AVENUE
BLENHEIM ROAD
PARK GROVE
MT STREET
CHARLES STREET
PARK STREET
ST JOHN'S ROAD
CASTLE STREET
DAY STREET
POND STREET
WALL STREET
DOBIE STREET
BEECH STREET
TUNE STREET
PINDAR OAKS STREET
COMMERCIAL STREET
FREEMAN STREET
SPENCER STREET

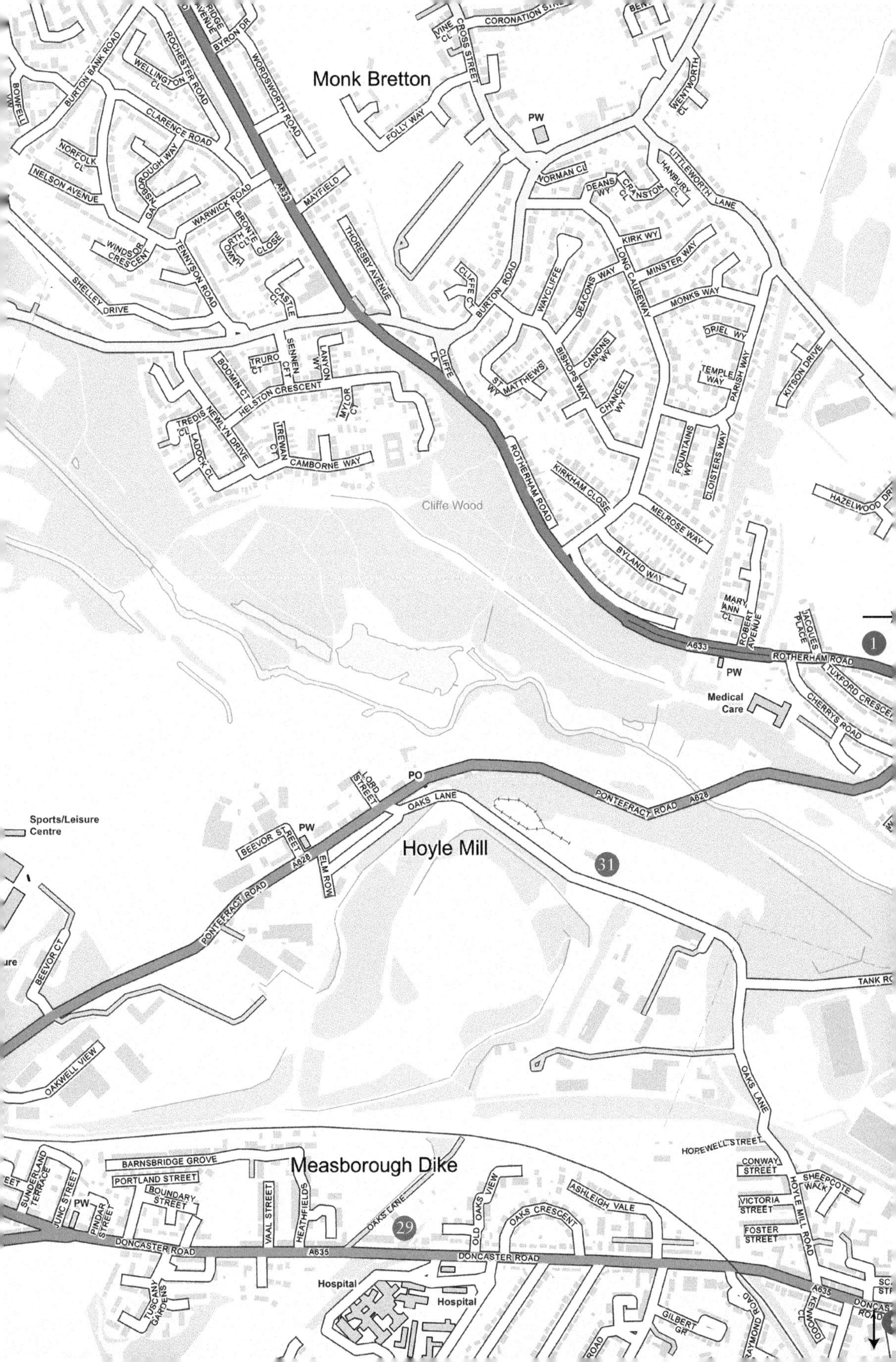

Monk Bretton
Hoyle Mill
Measborough Dike
Cliffe Wood
PW
PO
Medical Care
Sports/Leisure Centre
Hospital
A633
A628
A635
1
31
29
BURTON BANK ROAD
BOWFELL
WELLINGTON CL
ROCHESTER ROAD
WORDSWORTH ROAD
BYRON DR
CLARENCE ROAD
NORFOLK CL
NELSON AVENUE
ROUGH WAY
WARWICK ROAD
MAYFIELD
BRONTE CLOSE
WINDSOR CRESCENT
TENNYSON ROAD
SHELLEY DRIVE
CASTLE CL
THORESBY AVENUE
CORONATION STREET
VINE CL
CROSS STREET
FOLLY WAY
WENTWORTH CL
NORMAN CL
DEANS WY
CRANSTON CL
HANBURY CL
LITTLEWORTH LANE
KIRK WY
LONG CAUSEWAY
MINSTER WAY
DEACONS WAY
WAYCLIFFE
CLIFFE CT
BURTON ROAD
MONKS WAY
ORIEL WY
TEMPLE WAY
PARISH WAY
KITSON DRIVE
CANONS WY
BISHOPS WAY
CHANCEL WY
ST MATTHEWS WY
CLIFFE LA
SENNEN CFT
TRURO CT
LANYON WY
BODMIN CT
HELSTON CRESCENT
MYLOR CT
TREDIS CL
NEWLYN DRIVE
LADOCK CL
TREWAN CT
CAMBORNE WAY
ROTHERHAM ROAD
KIRKHAM CLOSE
FOUNTAINS WY
CLOISTERS WAY
HAZELWOOD DR
MELROSE WAY
BYLAND WAY
MARY ANN CL
ROBERT AVENUE
JACQUES PLACE
TUXFORD CRESCENT
CHERRYS ROAD
LORD STREET
OAKS LANE
PONTEFRACT ROAD
BEEVOR STREET
ELM ROW
BEEVOR CT
TANK ROW
OAKWELL VIEW
HOPEWELL STREET
CONWAY STREET
VICTORIA STREET
FOSTER STREET
SHEEPCOTE WALK
HOYLE MILL ROAD
BARNSBRIDGE GROVE
PORTLAND STREET
BOUNDARY STREET
SUNDERLAND TERRACE
JUNC STREET
PINDAR STREET
VAAL STREET
HEATHFIELDS
OLD OAKS VIEW
OAKS CRESCENT
ASHLEIGH VALE
DONCASTER ROAD
TUSCANY GARDENS
GILBERT GR
RAYMOND ROAD
KENWOOD CL

Key

1. The Mill of the Black Monks
2. St Mary's Church, Worsbrough
3. St Mary's Church, Barnsley
4. Nos 41–43 Church Street
5. Gunthwaite Barn
6. Cannon Hall, Museum Park and Gardens
7. Worsbrough Mill and Country Park
8. Newcomen Beam Engine
9. Wentworth Castle
10. White Bear (Royal Hotel)
11. The Old No. 7
12. The Victorian Arcade and George Yard
13. Cooper Gallery and Newman Bond Solicitors
14. The Lamproom Theatre and Pinfold Steps
15. Wesleyan Methodist Association Chapel
16. Temperance Hall
17. Former Coach and Horses and Peel Square North
18. The Chronicle Building and Peel Square South and East
19. The Courthouse
20. New Courthouse
21. The Queens Hotel
22. Locke Park Columns
23. Joseph Locke Monument
24. Penistone Viaduct
25. Locke Tower
26. The Bandstand
27. National Union of Mineworkers Offices
28. The Miners Hall
29. Kendray Monument
30. Oaks Colliery Disaster Memorial
31. Barnsley Main
32. The Former York Street Baths
33. The Civic Theatre
34. Oakwell Stadium
35. The Church of St Peter the Apostle and John the Baptist
36. Arcadia House and the Co-operative Buildings
37. Theatre Royal
38. National Westminster Bank
39. Former Barnsley Girls High School
40. Barnsley Town Hall
41. The War Memorial and Barnsley Pals Centenary Square
42. Mining and Technical College
43. Montague Burton Building
44. Parkway Cinema
45. John Rideal House
46. Transport Interchange
47. Barry Hines House
48. Barnsley College
49. Barnsley Sixth Form College
50. Lightbox and Glassworks

A Brief History of Barnsley

Barnsley made headline news in January 2003 when architect Will Alsop compared it to a Tuscan hill town, while a millennium earlier 'Berneslai' – 'barn in a field' – made it into the Domesday Book. Driven by Monk Bretton Priory, the town's epicentre moved to the top of Market Hill and a market charter was awarded in 1249 by Henry III.

In the thirteenth century, Barnsley's evolution was centred chiefly on agriculture. However, local coal meant farmers could burn less manure for fuel and coal ash mixed with lime supplied fertiliser. After the Dissolution of the Monasteries in 1541 there were 600 denizens.

Barnsley turned into a raucous port of call on the burgeoning seventeenth-century stagecoach and mail coach routes. Trade from travellers boosted coaching inns and Barnsley's reputation as a wicked place reached John Wesley's ears. In his *A Tour Through the Whole Island of Great Britain of 1724*, Daniel Defoe called the town 'Black Barnsley' due to the heathland setting, but he also noted that the town was 'black and smoaky as if they were all smiths that lived in it'.

To exploit Barnsley's vast coal reserves construction of the Barnsley Canal was approved by Parliament in 1793. Adversely affected by low water supply and subsidence from mining, Barnsley Canal closed in 1953. Although little remains, names such as Lock Keeper's Gate are still being applied.

A population explosion took place, in part due to reduced fear of the plague, allowing rapid urbanisation, but also from the growth of coal mining and expanding railway networks. In 1960, there were seventy collieries within a 15-mile radius of Barnsley town centre, but the last of these closed in 1994.

Besides coal mining, Barnsley was one of Britain's principal centres for the manufacture of linen and glass. In 1744, Cheshire-based Quaker William Wilson chose to produce linen yarn in Barnsley to be woven across the Pennines. William's nephew, Joseph Beckett, known as the father of the Barnsley linen industry, encouraged weavers to settle in Barnsley. Weavers' cottages were built, and at Town End water provided by the Sough Dyke meant dark mills with their ponds clustered.

Barnsley's coat of arms depicts a glassblower and a miner. Ben Rylands opened Hope Glassworks in 1867 and formed a partnership with Hiram Codd in 1877 to produce the Codd Bottle for fizzy drinks. A marble in the neck of the bottle was pushed up by the pressure of the carbon dioxide. The screw-top wine bottle was patented by Dan Rylands in 1889 and in 1977 local man Stanley Race made the first deposit in a bottle bank in the United Kingdom.

During the twentieth century the ball and chain and occasional fire meant most of the weavers' cottages and linen mills vanished. A former linen warehouse on the corner of St Mary's Place and Churchfield is one of the few reminders of this heritage. New civic buildings replaced much of the medieval settlement, but despite occasional modernist missteps and the loss of some fine buildings there are many signs of an enormously well-healed past with oodles of cash available for boaster buildings.

The 50 Buildings

1. The Mill of the Black Monks

The Mill of the Black Monks, 2 miles east of Barnsley town centre, is closely associated with the haunting ruins of the Cluniac order Monk Bretton Priory of St Mary Magdalene of Lund. Monasteries on a grand scale were a common sight in medieval times, there being over sixty in Yorkshire. Abbey churches would tower above the adjacent medieval settlements.

A mill was included within the land given to the monks by Adam Fitzswain of Silkstone in 1154. Recently discovered evidence confirms that a Saxon mill existed on the site of this unique public house with thirteenth-century origins.

The mill was powered by water brought by a leat or open watercourse from the River Dearne. A large stone drain took water to the priory, where it flushed the refectory and a reredorter or communal latrine and then returned it to the leat. The priory ruins include the south wall of the monks' refectory and a network of well-preserved drains.

On the heels of the Dissolution of the Monasteries in 1589 Monk Bretton Priory was purchased by George Talbot, the Earl of Shrewsbury, for his son,

View of the Mill of the Black Monks from Pontefract Road.

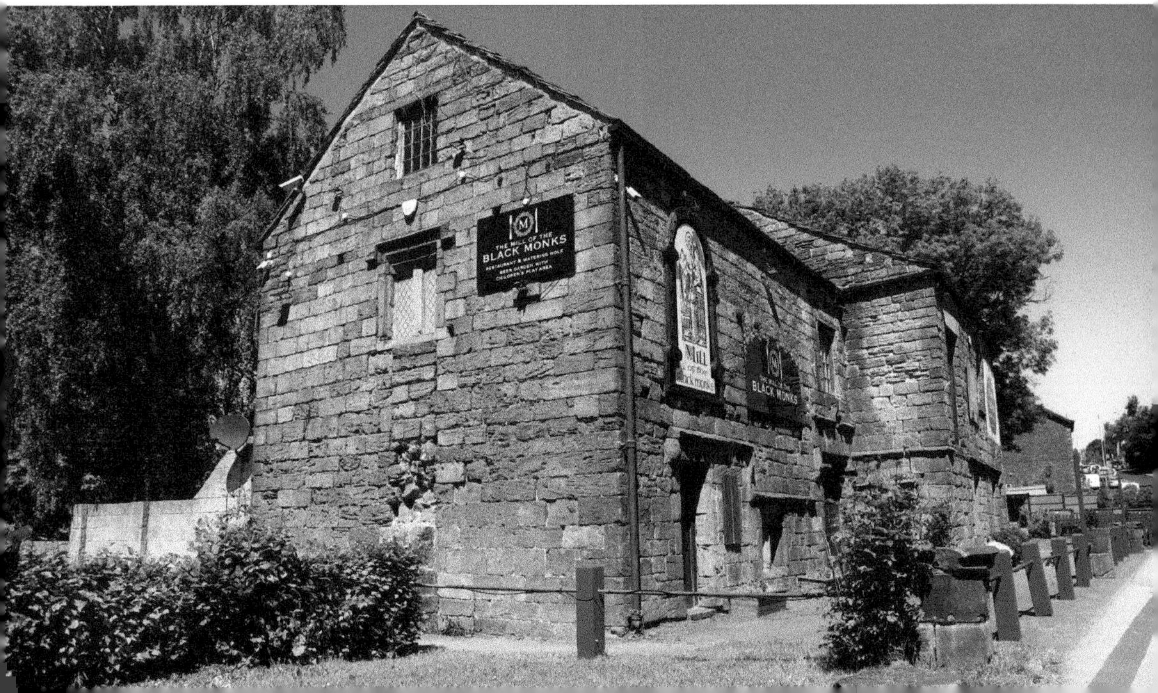

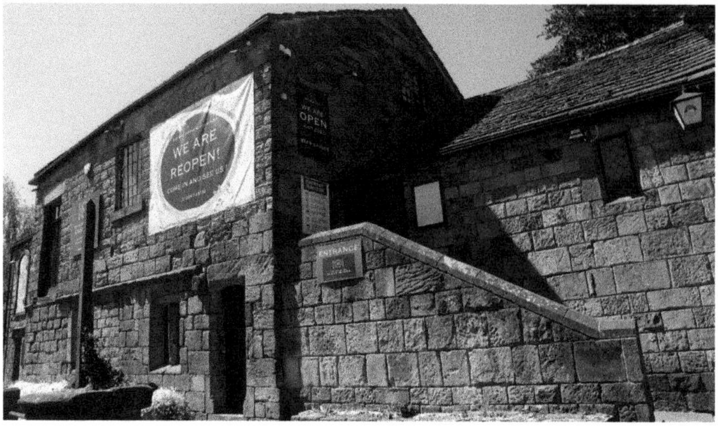

Among the numerous inscriptions recorded is one from 1709 by a previous miller, Ralf Taylor.

Henry. Archaeological surveys show a grand Tudor house was created within the cloisters by George Talbot, who was one of Elizabeth I's leading noblemen and one of the richest and most powerful men in the country. At Elizabeth's request he took custody of Mary, Queen of Scots as his 'guest' for fifteen years (1569–84).

The priory mill was extensively modernised in 1635 by Sir William Armyne, a baronet and leading MP from Lincolnshire who supported Parliament in the Civil War. His second wife, Mary, was the daughter of Henry Talbot. Among many charitable acts, Mary Armyne provided a row of six almshouses for the poor next to the mill.

Falling within the bottomlands around the River Deane seasonal high-water discharges caused a gradual build-up of silt around the mill over the centuries. The compromised building was being used as a store and in danger of demolition when the current owner, an architect and archaeologist, hydraulically lifted and renovated the building. It was this extraordinary restoration that revealed the remains of the previous seventh-century Saxon mill, including internal and external inscriptions and original parts dating from around AD 650.[1]

2. St Mary's Church, Worsbrough

This Grade I listed church is part of an attractive unified group with a sixteenth-century house and attached school, now used as church rooms. St Mary's contains stonework with Saxon origins. The chancel is from Norman times and other parts date from the fourteenth and fifteenth centuries. The south door, which has a Gothic inscription, dates from 1480.

At the north entrance there is a squire or family box pew with a panelled screen and seventeenth-century brasses. This was the Elmhirst family pew and records show that William Elmehyrste and William Broddesworth opened a grammar school here in 1560. The Elmhirst family lived at Houndhill, a manor house located south-west of Barnsley, which dates from around 1566. The family tree includes

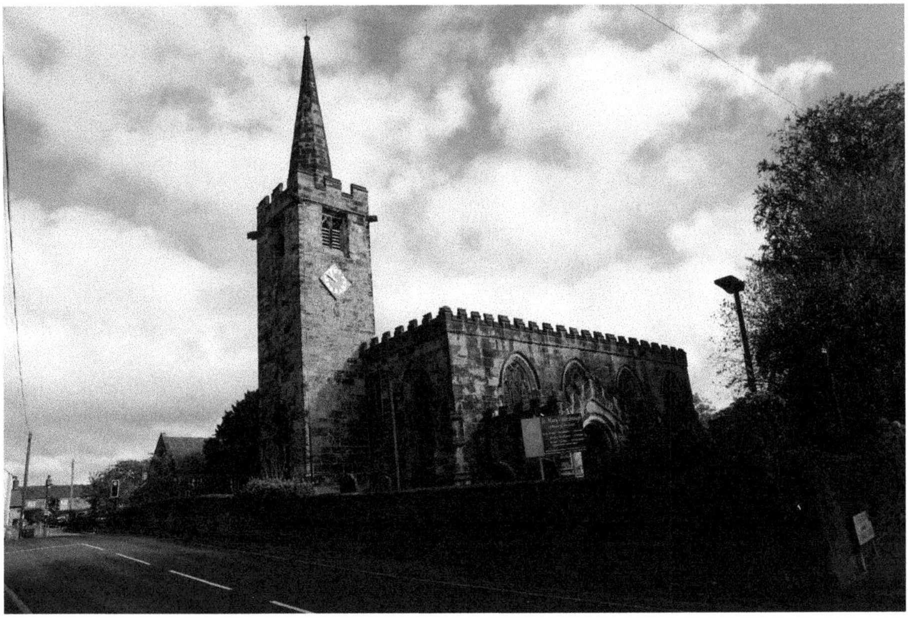

The church is opposite the Edmunds Arms and near to Worsbrough Hall.

many notable people, including Air Vice Marshall Sir Thomas Elmhirst, who was knighted for distinguished service during the First and Second world wars.

However, the most unique feature is a double-decker oak tomb with a cadaver on the lower bunk and a knight on top. This is the burial place of Sir Roger Rockley, who died in 1533.The Rockley family has a long association with Worsbrough. Sir Robert Rockley also has a monument in the church. He fought with John of Gaunt, Duke of Lancaster, son of Edward III and father of Henry IV. Sir Robert was elected to the House of Commons in 1402.[2]

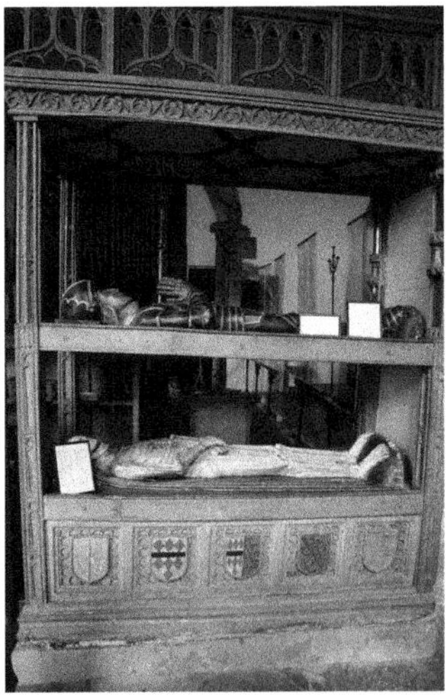

The double-decker monument to Sir Roger Rockley.

The church was remodelled in 1838 by York-based architect J. P. Prichett, whose most famous work would probably be the Grade I listed Huddersfield railway station. The east window is by renowned painted- and stained-glass maker William Wailes and dates from 1846. In the nineteenth century many fourteenth-century churches were repaired. However, often this meant rebuilding to an idealised view of what a church should look like. Pevsner says St Mary's was severely altered, resulting in a general heightening.

The church, which has a recessed octagonal spire protruding from a square tower, is set in attractive walled grounds. The graveyard includes two chest tombs surrounded by iron railings and many graves of historic interest. This is where most of the seventy-five miners killed in the Darley Main Colliery Disaster on 24 January 1849 are buried in five unmarked graves. At the funeral service it was said that the church could scarcely accommodate the families of the deceased.

3. St Mary's Church, Barnsley

A church has stood on this site since Saxon times; however, in the fourteenth century the church was rebuilt in the Romanesque style. It was an important feature of the early town and was described in the *Gentleman's Magazine* in the early nineteenth century as a beautiful piece of Norman work.

The impact of the French Revolution and rapid urbanisation meant the influence of the Established Church was waning. To meet the new population's spiritual needs, the Church Buildings Act of 1818 resulted in 214 Waterloo churches. In the early nineteenth century all but the tower of the previous Romanesque church

View from the Peace Gardens, which were once the burial ground for the church.

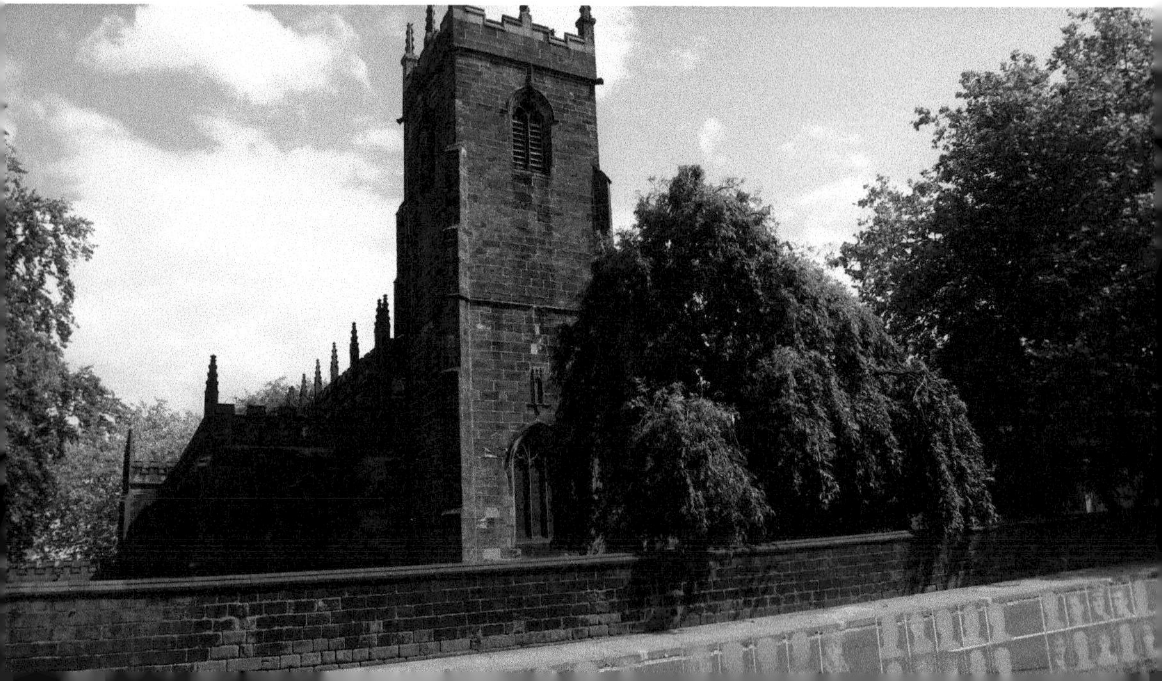

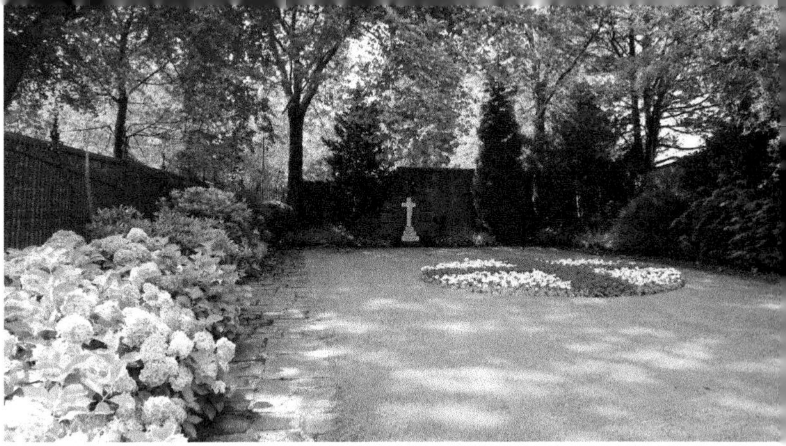

The memorial garden was given to the church by Samuel Cooper.

was demolished. The Gothic body of a new church, designed by Thomas Rickman, was added to the retained tower. The new church was consecrated in 1822.

Rickman was a Quaker and, coincidentally, the Barnsley Quaker meeting house, which contains gravestones dating from 1688, is located nearby on Huddersfield Road. Rickman had started out in medicine but wrote the seminal work *An Attempt to Discriminate the Styles of English Architecture from the Conquest to the Reformation* (1817). In this Rickman described early Gothic as 'Decorated' and late Gothic as 'Perpendicular' – terms that are still used.

The interior of St Mary's Church was restored around 1870 by another leading light of Gothic Revival, George Frederick Bodley, who was also a poet and musician. Bodley's style, which was termed 'English Decorated Gothic', influenced the interiors of many churches.

The church contains numerous memorials to the most prosperous and influential families in Barnsley. Another Quaker, Joseph Beckett, was regarded as a founding father of the linen trade. After his death in 1840 a marble monument was placed in the south chancel of St Mary's Church. Joseph's son, John Staniforth Beckett, was the founder of the Beckett Dispensary (1865). Beckett Hospital was a very imposing structure; all that is left now is a metal plaque opposite St Mary's Church.

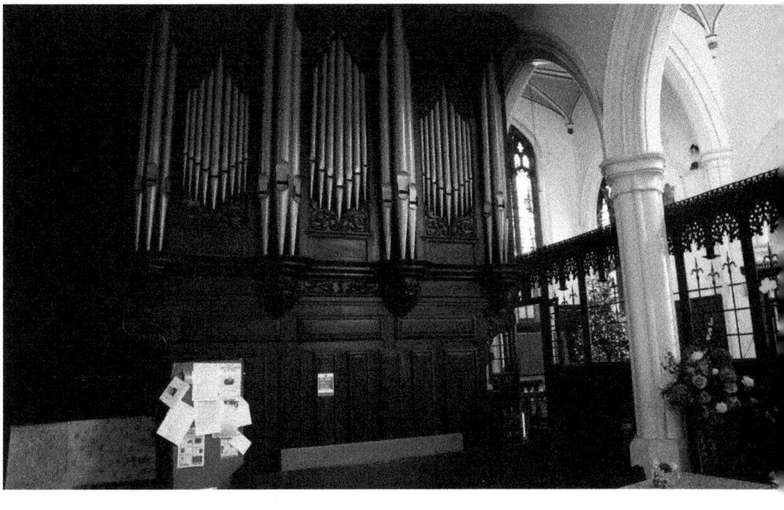

The Father Smith Organ Case. Bernard Smith was organ builder to Charles II.

4. Nos 41–43 Church Street

These timber-framed buildings opposite St Mary's Church are some of the few remaining medieval town houses in Barnsley. First erected as a fifteenth-century hall in 1455, a cross wing was added at right angles to the original house in 1464. When the Cluniac monks moved the town into this area local timber was readily available and used widely for new buildings. However, timber was being used for fuel, shipbuilding and many other types of construction. At the same time land was also being cleared for agriculture and as land covered by woodlands reduced timber became scarce, meaning that by the middle of the seventeenth century stone buildings started to predominate.

In the early eighteenth century, Church Street was one of the busiest streets in Barnsley. Its buildings were altered due to the realignment of Church Street in the mid-eighteenth century. This included significant changes to internal floor levels and the insertion of a cellar level. Two bays of the fifteenth-century hall were also removed.

The rear elevation to Richardson's yard provides the best external view of the original timber frame, timber mullioned window and the brick-walled cellar level. Old maps show that this yard contained the town's mortuary. Another fine building that once stood to the south on Church Street was Deputy House. The former house of Samuel Cooper was named after its last occupant, the National Association of Colliery Deputies and Shotfirers (NACODS).

When Beckett Hospital relocated a florist closed down and in 1969 the shop was occupied by landscape artist and TV personality Ashley Jackson. He extended into the adjacent art and gift shop, which served the nearby Barnsley College of Art that Jackson himself had attended.[3] Ashley Jackson's shop was closed in 2011 and is now occupied by an estate agent.

In August 2002, restoration took place, which was funded by the owners of the building (*Barnsley Chronicle*) in association with English Heritage and Barnsley Council. The restoration replaced badly decayed timbers. The original timbers

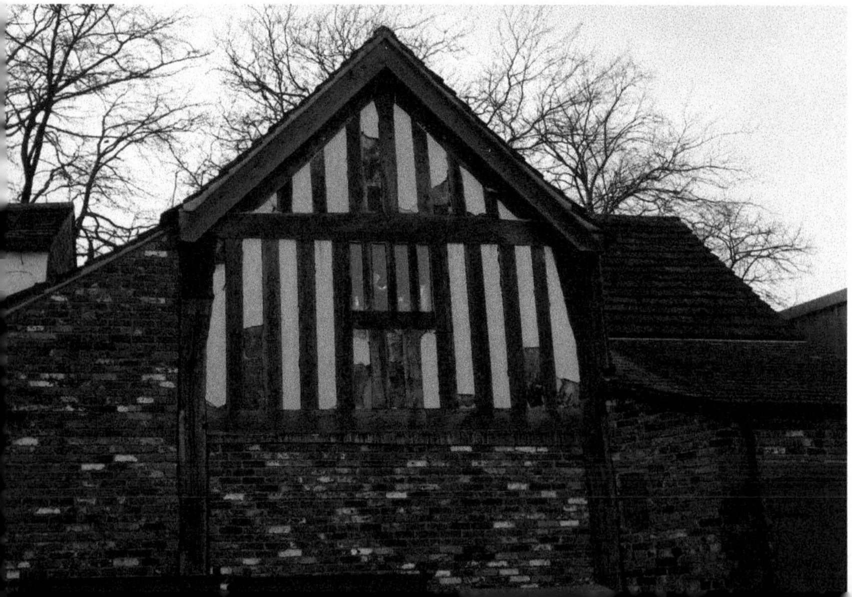

The projecting end gable of the cross wing shows the timber frame.

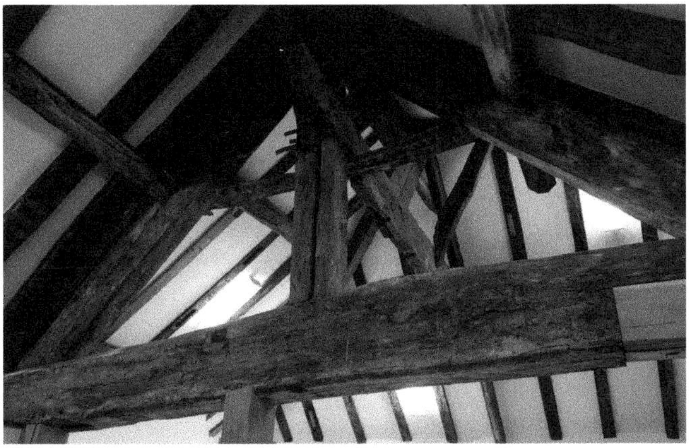
Medieval timbers can be seen inside the estate agents that currently occupy the building.

used in the construction of the building were also dated and found to be from between 1455 and 1479. Medieval timbers were also discovered in the former Butterfield and Massey's store opposite the Town Hall.

5. Gunthwaite Barn

Barns from the sixteenth century are exceptionally rare and those that are still operating are of particular importance. Historic England regard this to be an excellent and unique complete working barn, and it holds a Grade I listing. This cruck barn, which is now in shared ownership, forms part of an attractive group of fine stone buildings. The adjacent stable range and farm buildings date from 1699 and 1701 respectively. The original timber-framed wood and plaster Gunthwaite Hall was demolished in the nineteenth century, but to the south of the 'new hall' is a summer house dated 1688.

The barn, which is still in agricultural use, is held together by wooden pegs.

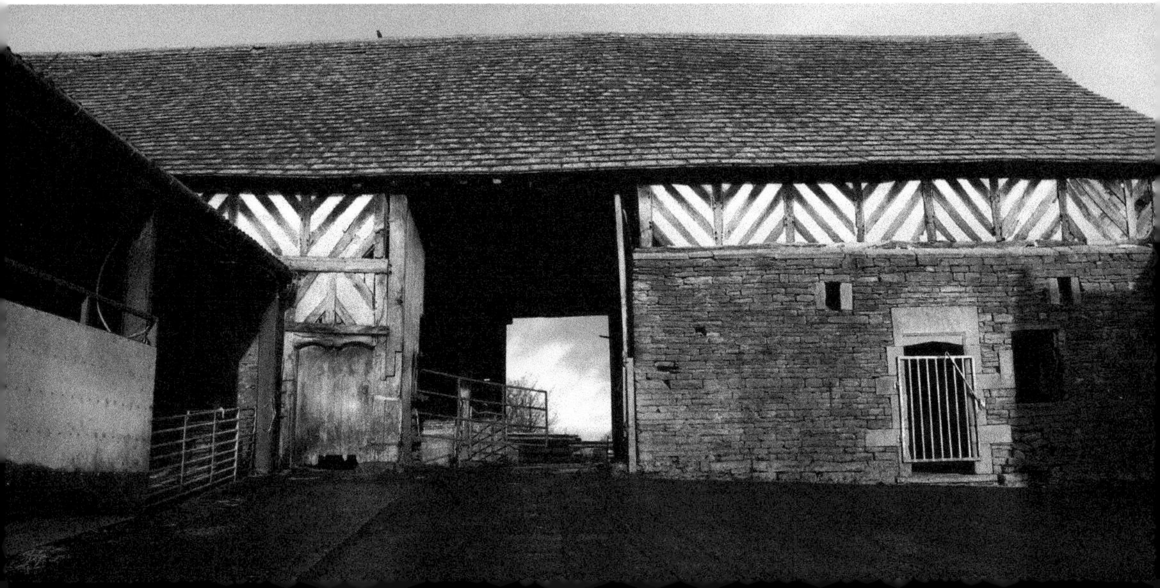

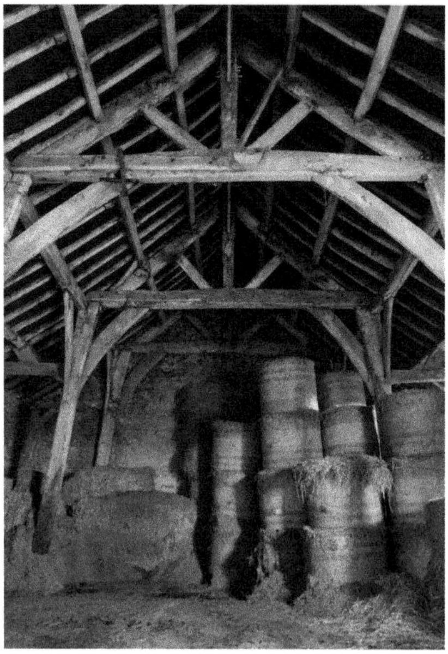

There are twelve king-post trusses with struts arch-braced to the ridge and six large barn doors.

The barn has a distinctive timber-framed band below the eaves of a stone slate roof supported by twenty-four original wooden pillars. These have remained intact because they stand on stone bases. There are large, opposing, full-height, square cart doors within the coursed, squared, rubble lower walls. Opposing doors are usually associated with a threshing floor with chaff caught by the cross draught.

Gunthwaite Barn was built in 1545 by Godfrey Bosville. The Bosville family have a long association with Gunthwaite Hall. Sir Martin de Bosville was a Norman knight who fought with William the Conqueror at the Battle of Hastings. The family originally lived at New Hall (now Cranford Hall) in Ardsley. Richard Bosville moved to Gunthwaite Hall in 1443 from a previous building on the site of what is now Cannon Hall.[4]

Another Godfrey Bosville was a Member of Parliament and Roundhead commander who fought against Charles I at Warwick Castle in 1642. His soldiers would stay in the barn, but on one such visit many fell ill and died. It is said that these soldiers were buried under an oak tree nearby.

Elizabeth Diana Bosville married Alexander MacDonald. The Bosville-MacDonalds owned Thorpe Hall at Rudston, near Bridlington, and this became their main residence, leading to the demolition of the Tudor Gunthwaite Hall.

A sulphur-rich spring called Gunthwaite Spa is set in a stone recess by the side of Carr Lane. On Spaw Sunday (the first Sunday in May) thousands of people would come from miles around to an annual festival with food and drink stalls and musicians playing. Benedictine monks would attend, and the Abbot of Pontefract blessed the waters, which had alleged medicinal qualities due to its high silver content. These festivities ceased around 1870 when crowds grew too large and anti-social behaviour became a problem.

6. Cannon Hall, Museum Park and Gardens

Cannon Hall overlooks sloping land immediately north-west of the historic village of Cawthorne. The village is connected to the hall via an attractive path that crosses a bridge built in 1762 and meanders through parkland.

While the land was recorded in the Domesday Book of 1086 as containing a manor house, it is the thirteenth-century house owned by Gilbert Canun that gives the hall its name. In 1764–68, Cannon Hall was remodelled by Horbury-born architect John Carr. Cannon Hall offers museums, 70 acres of historic parkland, formal gardens and a working farm as a separate award-winning visitor attraction.

The terrace along the south wall of the hall looks out over a manicured landscape that draws the visitor's eye to the hall. A front door here would have been exposed to winds from across the valley. A ha-ha marks the transition from formal gardens to parklands, which once contained deer that used a shelter close to the hall. The Cannon Hall Country Park contains many fascinating buildings, including the Camelia House, hot house and hot wall, which held fireplaces to help grow a wide variety of fruits. A restful walled pear garden with two conservatories is accessed by a round, arched, gated entrance.

Before Barnsley Council acquired the site in 1951, Cannon Hall was the home of the Spencer-Stanhope family, who made their fortune in the local iron and coal industries. One of the most interesting was Walter Spencer-Stanhope, who

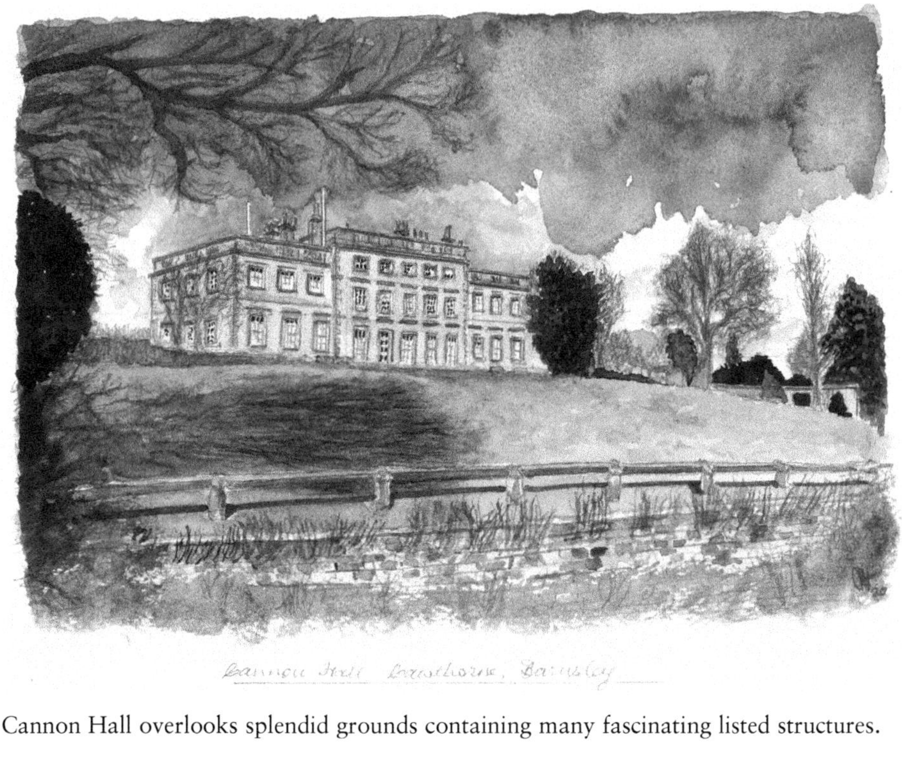

Cannon Hall overlooks splendid grounds containing many fascinating listed structures.

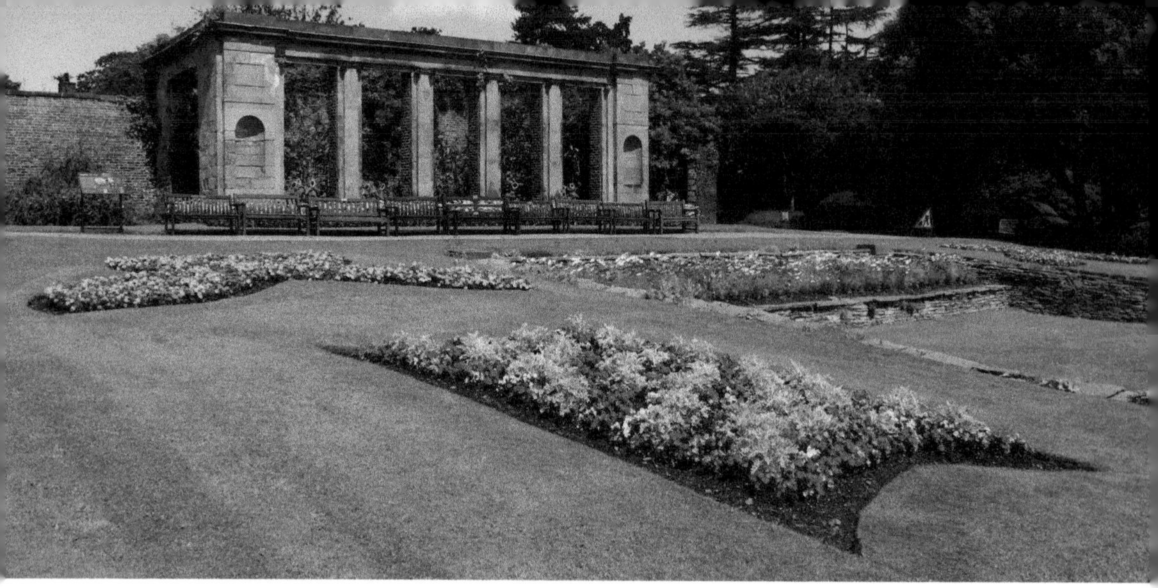

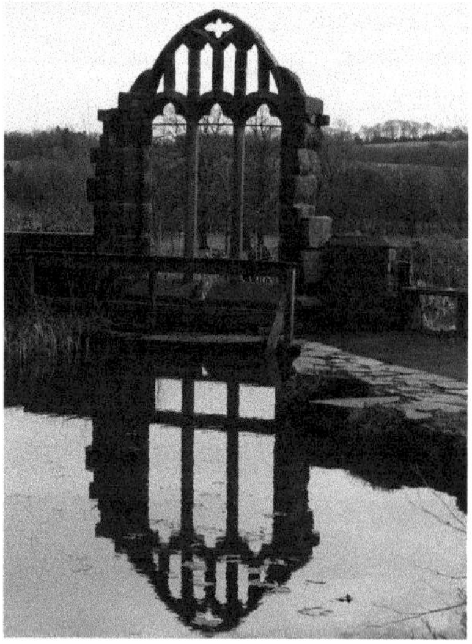

Above: Camelia house, the hot wall and hot house, behind which is a walled pear garden.

Left: A sixteenth-century Gothic arch was taken from a local church.

inherited the hall in 1775. As a Tory MP he became friends with Independent MP William Wilberforce, the anti-slavery campaigner. William Wilberforce visited Cannon Hall on several occasions.

On 15 October 1792, Walter Spencer Stanhope attended a public subscription meeting at the White Bear Hotel (later to become the Royal Hotel) and became the principal shareholder and chairman for the Barnsley Canal Company. He owned land that contained the Silkstone coal seam, and when the canal opened in 1799 a spur passed close to Cannon Hall. The canal, with connections to Worsbrough Mill and Elsecar, would be a key factor in Barnsley's industrial development.

The Cannon Hall Museum includes sumptuous rooms, artwork by John Constable and Chippendale furniture. A separate museum is dedicated to the Royal Hussars and the Light Dragoons. Their history includes Dunkirk and D-Day. They were also part of the front line of the Charge of the Light Brigade.[5]

7. Worsbrough Mill and Country Park

This working flour mill and museum is set in 240 acres of superb parkland within the valley of the River Dove. The miller's cottage, which dates from the eighteenth century, is now the museum offices. Millers such as Fred Watson and Reg Steel lived and worked here for decades. Skilled stone dressers were needed to cut the precise grooves in the stones used to grind the wheat. Barnsley Museums Film Archive from 1977 shows stone dresser Thomas Devey working on a French Burr millstone he first created in 1925. The mill is powered by a nineteenth-century bucket waterwheel driving three pairs of millstones.

The original two-storey section of Worsbrough Mill dates from the seventeenth century, but flour milling in the valley dates back over 900 years. The mill is thought to have been built around 1625 during the reign of Charles I, who is said to have visited the nearby Worsbrough Hall during the Civil War. While the original mill is water powered, the attached three-storey building (dating from around 1843) had a steam-powered mill.

Prior to the Industrial Revolution there were thousands of similar small water- and wind-powered flour mills. Horse and cart transport meant they were located only 10–15 miles apart. With the coming of canals and railways, bigger steam-driven mills were made possible. Coal for the steam boiler, as well as the wheat for milling, could be delivered easily and cheaply, putting the smaller water mills out of business.

The original seventeenth-century water mill is attached to a three-storey, nineteenth-century extension.

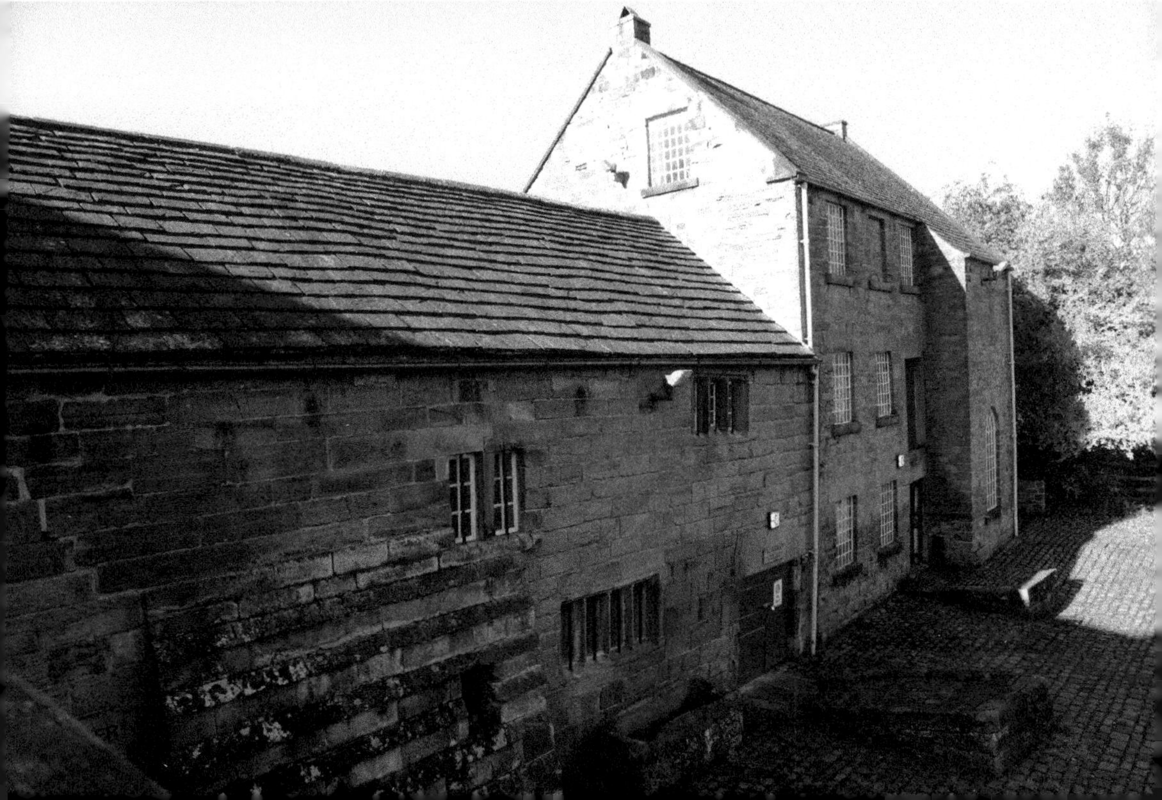

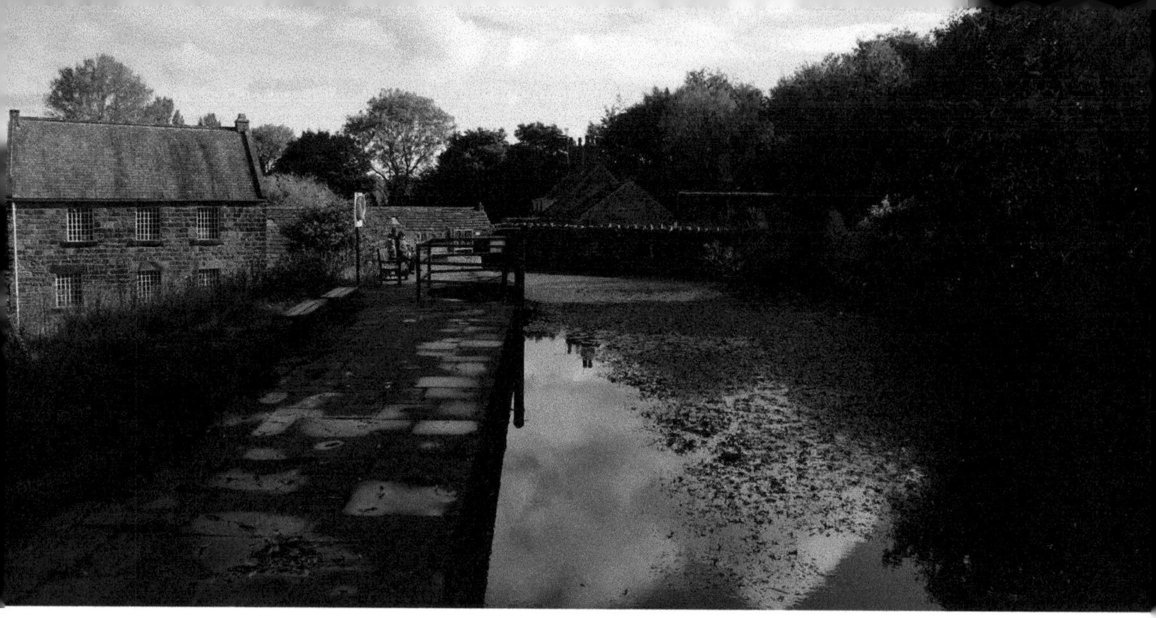

A sandstone bridge dating from 1809 provides views of the millpond.

Worsbrough Mill became run down and severe storms in the 1950s caused significant structural deterioration. There are now only around thirty other traditional flour mills in the country. The mill was restored and opened to the public in 1976 by the South Yorkshire County Council and now produces high-quality, slow-ground, organic flour and supplies many artisan bakeries around the country. Worsbrough produces around 17 tonnes of flour per year and was featured on *Countryfile*.

Among the events held at the mill is an annual ghost walk on Halloween. Actors hosting the event recount unexplained paranormal activities at the mill from centuries past. It is claimed to be one of Barnsley's most haunted locations.

8. Newcomen Beam Engine

The Elsecar Heritage Centre offers a unique manifestation of the Industrial Revolution, with transport, coal mining, an ironworks and workers' houses in one setting.

The first shaft of Elsecar New Colliery was sunk in 1794 and the Elsecar Ironworks opened in 1795. Skilled craftsmen such as carpenters, clock and instrument makers drove the Industrial Revolution. To extract coal from deep mines it was essential to pump out huge quantities of water. Blacksmith Thomas Newcomen (1664–1729) invented the first practical solution for tin mines in his native Devon. Newcomen's design was used for over fifty years in hundreds of deep mines across the country. First applied to coal extraction in 1712, his steam engine used a condensing cylinder to create a vacuum. Atmospheric pressure and a weighted beam produced a circular motion that pushed water out of a dedicated shaft.

Elsecar's 'great engine' was built by John Bargh from Chesterfield but was subsequently modified and improved. In 1836, the locally grown wooden beam

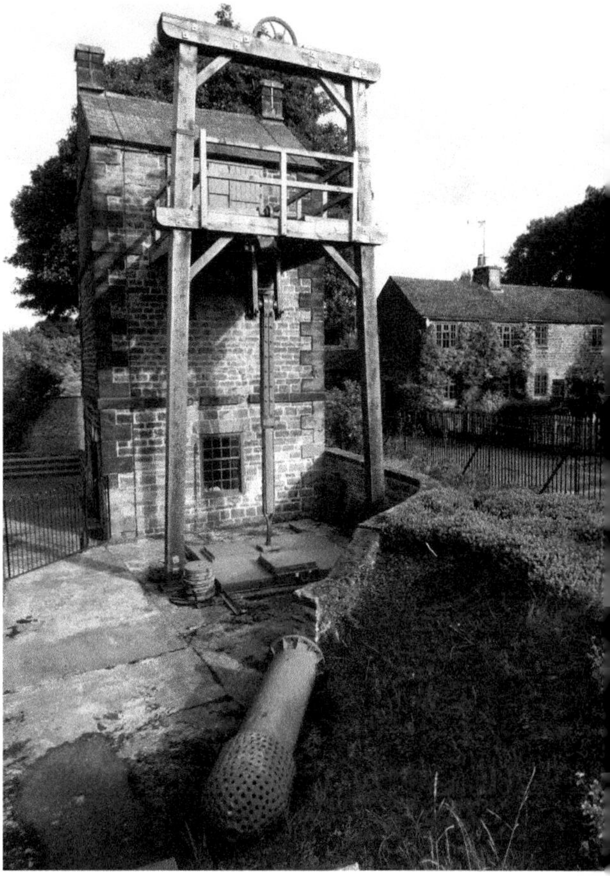

Right: A recent archaeological dig uncovered brick-lined boiler pits dating from around 1850.

Below: The colliery closed in 1984 and the industrial heritage centre now includes artisan businesses, cafés and shops.

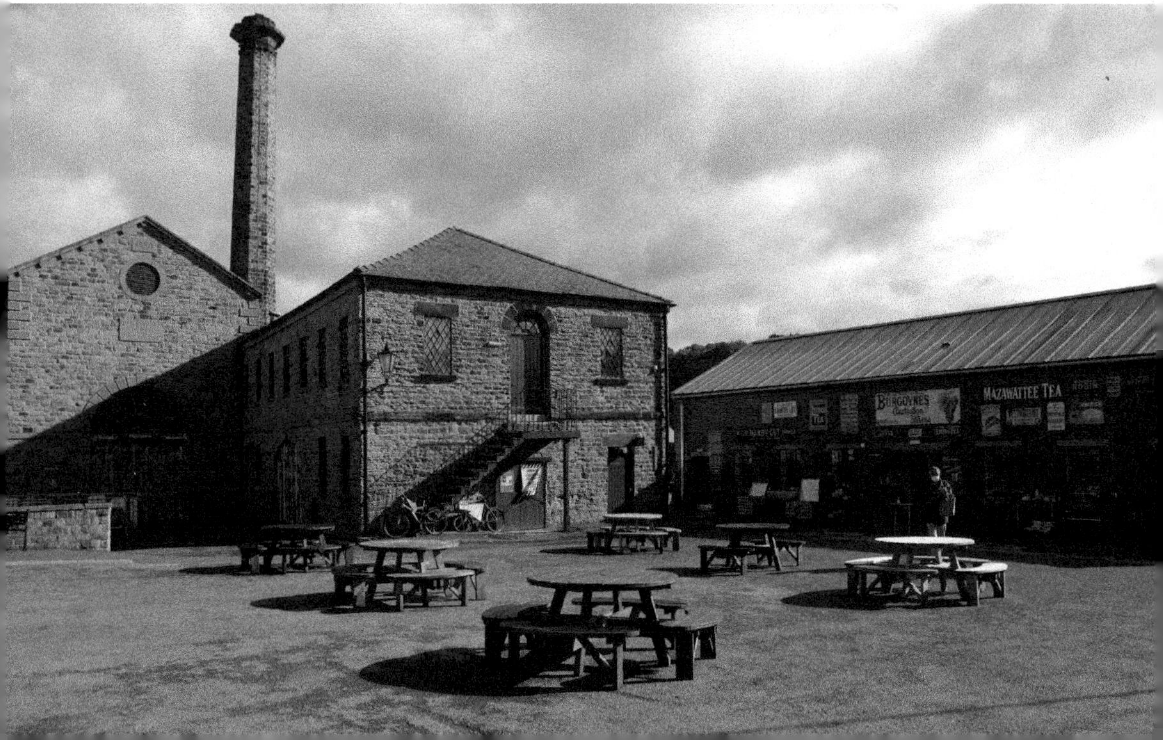

was replaced with an iron beam fitted with parallel motion invented by James Watt in 1784. Watt had studied Newcomen's design and initially refined it by contriving a second condenser.

The Newcomen engine was still in full-time use in 1923 and was then retained for back-up use and needed for this purpose in 1928. The engine has been restored and while a Newcomen beam engine can be seen elsewhere – such as at the inventor's birthplace of Dartmouth – at Elsecar the engine is in its original location, next to the railway station and sidings.

The former industrial buildings and railway are associated with those parts of Elsecar developed by William, the 4th Earl of Fitzwilliam (1748–1833), and his successors. The earls of Fitzwilliam lived at the palatial Wentworth Woodhouse, near Rotherham.

Mine owners had railed against trade unionism and firmly believed miners should rely upon the generosity of their patronage. At the start of 1912 the first 'great coal strike' had sought to establish the principle of a minimum wage. On 10 July 1912, George V visited Elsecar Main Colliery with William, the 7th Earl Fitzwilliam. The royal visit was overshadowed as ninety-one miners and rescue workers had died at Cadeby Colliery, near Doncaster, on the previous day.

9. Wentworth Castle

On the western edge of Barnsley, this fine stately home has direct family connections to Wentworth Woodhouse and is now a Grade I registered landscape. The 1st Earl of Strafford, who owned the Wentworth Woodhouse estate, was a leading supporter of Charles I. Parliament voted for his execution in 1641 and his honours and estates were confiscated. Thomas Wentworth had hoped to inherit his great-uncle's estate, but in 1695 it passed to the Watson-Wentworth side of the family and a fierce rivalry developed.

In 1708, Thomas purchased Stainborough Hall and remodelled it to create Wentworth Castle in the hope that it would help him restore the Strafford earldom. While British envoy to Prussia, he asked Johann von Bodt to design the east wing in a Franco-Prussian style.[6] In 1711, the earldom was briefly recreated by Queen Anne, but in 1802 the title finally became extinct. Overlooking Wentworth Castle on the Worsbrough Ridgeway walk, 'the High Stone' has carvings from 1756 believed to be dedicated to the Earl of Strafford.

The Vernon-Wentworth family continued ownership until 1948. The coal mines and farmland on the estate provided vast amounts of money and Frederick Vernon-Wentworth invested heavily in the parkland and gardens. The spectacular tree-lined approach to Stainborough Castle and the Serpentine lake are just some of the features in the impressive country house gardens.

After the reign of William and Mary the formal Dutch style predominated. Later gardens had woodlands with paths leading to clearings with sculptures

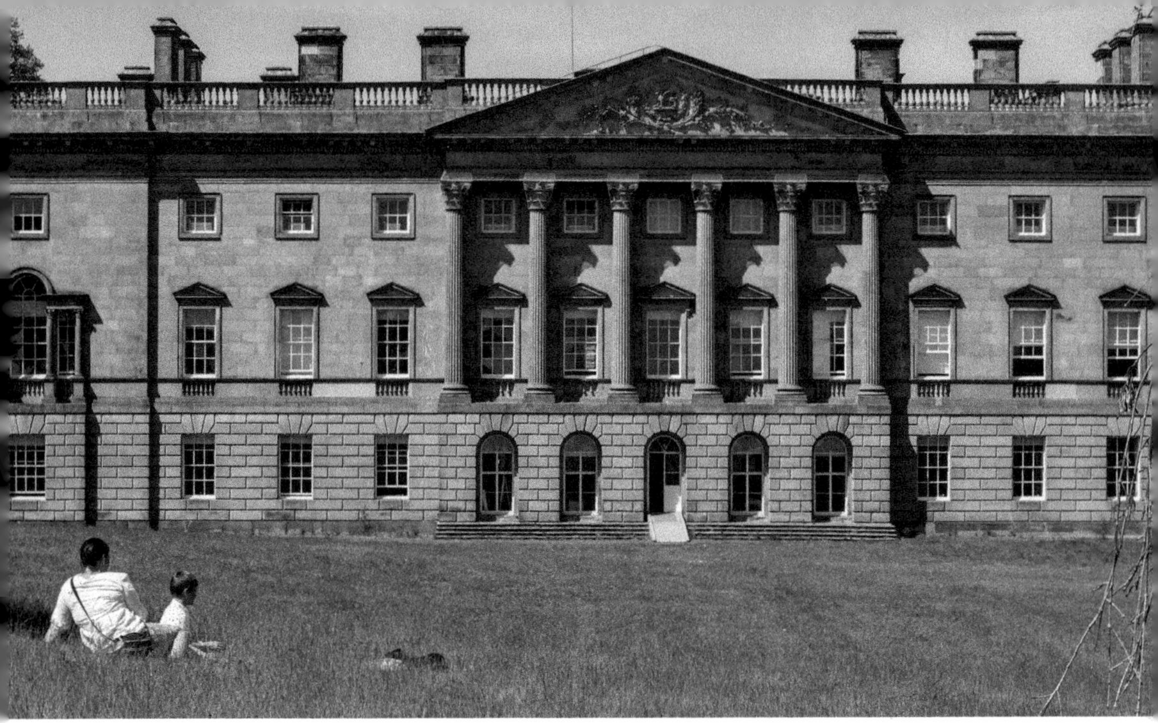

Parts of the castle date from when it was owned by Sir Gervase Cutler II. (© National Trust Images/Chris Lacey)

and temples, and there are twenty-six listed buildings within the grounds of Wentworth Castle.

Inheriting a considerable fortune from Frederick, his son Thomas added a Victorian conservatory built by Compton & Fawkes in 1886. The 'Iron Winter Garden' had electric lighting and underfloor heating and was used to grow exotic plants. In Victorian times the erection of such a large conservatory was an expression of wealth and status and prompted a royal visit by Prince Albert Victor, who could have been king had he not died during the flu pandemic of

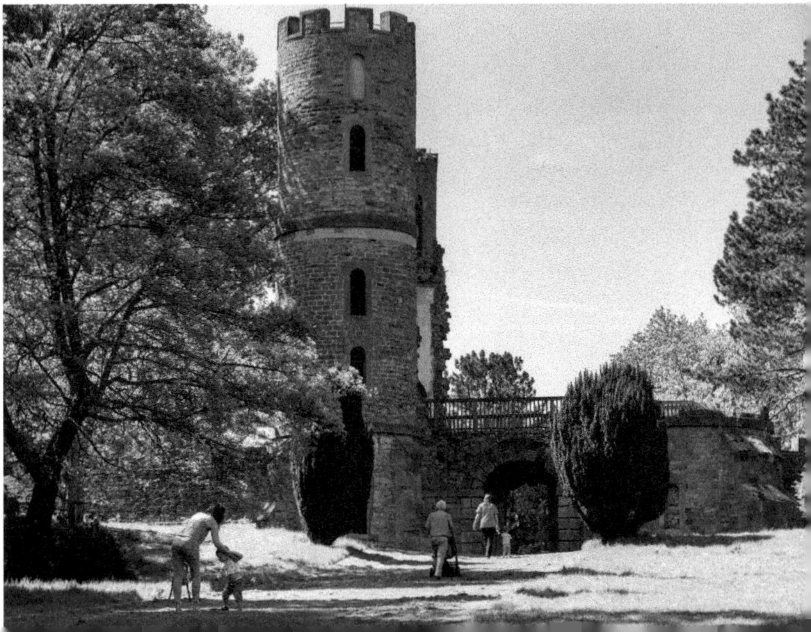

Stainborough Castle, a Gothic folly built in 1728–30. (© National Trust Images/Chris Lacey)

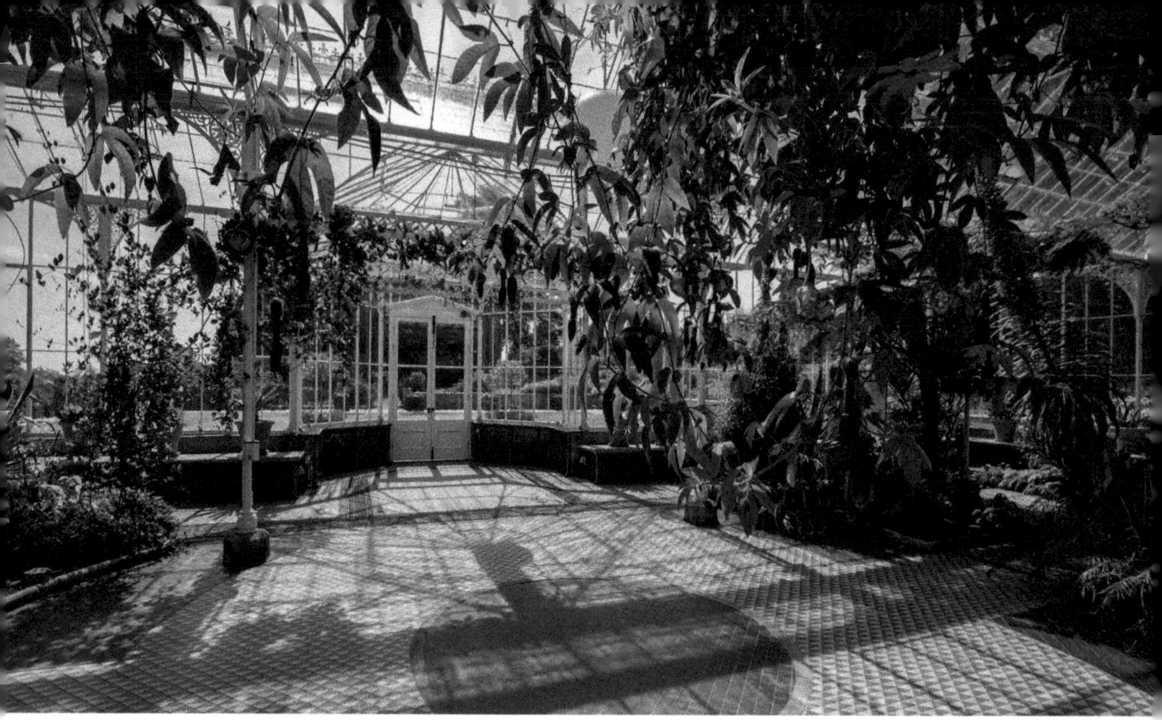

The winter gardens allowed Far Eastern camellias, rhododendrons and magnolias to be grown. (© National Trust Images/Chris Lacey)

1889–92. The unfortunate prince was perhaps most famous for being fallaciously accused of being Jack the Ripper.

Thomas died in 1902 and Captain Bruce Vernon Wentworth vacated the house and auctioned off the furniture, paintings and tapestries at Christies in 1919. During the Second World War, Wentworth Castle was used to house prisoners of war and it is now an adult training college. The National Trust have worked closely with the council and college to restore and reopen the grounds to the public.

10. White Bear (Royal Hotel)

Originally called the White Bear, this is a distinctive Georgian building of seven bays and three storeys. This eighteenth-century coaching inn was built in a prime position for travellers and residents, especially on market and fair days. Stagecoach companies established a route between London and York at the beginning of the eighteenth century and Barnsley benefited from being a convenient stopping point.

A stagecoach travelled in stages of between 10 and 15 miles, and the number of coaching inns grew significantly. At a stage stop, horses would be changed and travellers would have a meal, drink and maybe an overnight stay. Mail was also carried by coach, so it is not surprising that the former post office was located next to the White Bear.

Coaching inns can be recognised by the archways that allowed the coaches to pass through into the stable yard behind the inn. The partially blocked original arched entrance can be seen to the left of the White Bear.

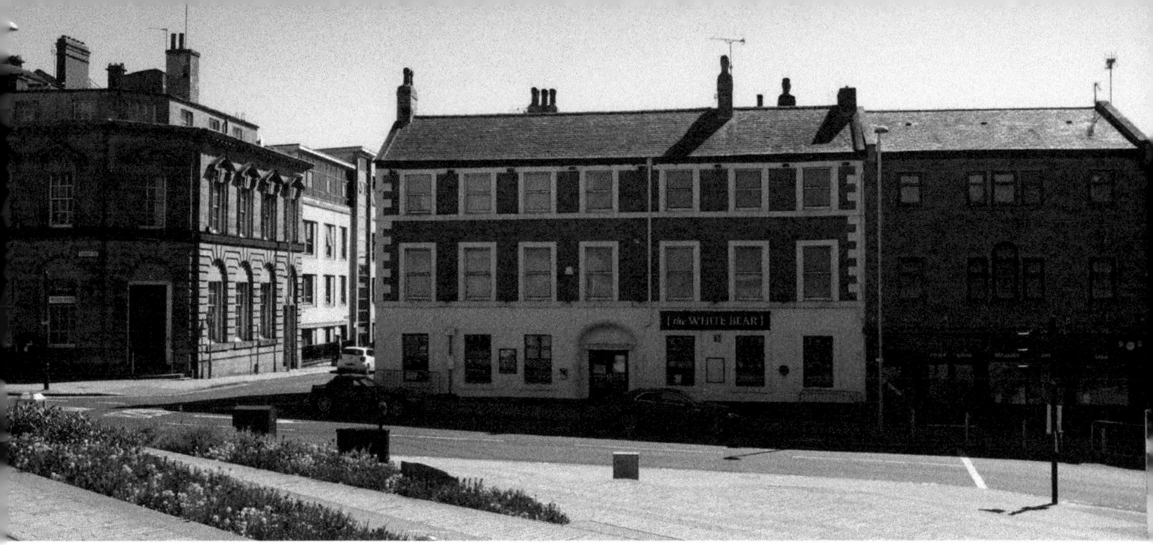

This Georgian public house is overlooked by the new public space next to the Town Hall.

The White Bear was renamed the Royal Hotel after a visit by Princess Victoria. She was travelling in a stagecoach from Wentworth Woodhouse with the Duchess of Kent on 14 September 1835. The royal coach was passing through Barnsley on the way to Harewood House and stopped at the White Bear for refreshment and fresh horses. Almost a century later the Prince of Wales opened the Town Hall, and his lunch of Barnsley chop, chips and peas was prepared at the Royal Hotel.[7]

The development of the railways led to the end of stagecoaches and mail coaches, which could not compete with the speed of the new railways. By the early 1840s many London-based mail coaches were being withdrawn from service. However, as Cudworth Station served Barnsley a horse-bus service was required until the opening of Court House station in 1870. The horse-bus was boarded at the Royal Hotel.

The building of the Town Hall required the loss of much of the original street scene.

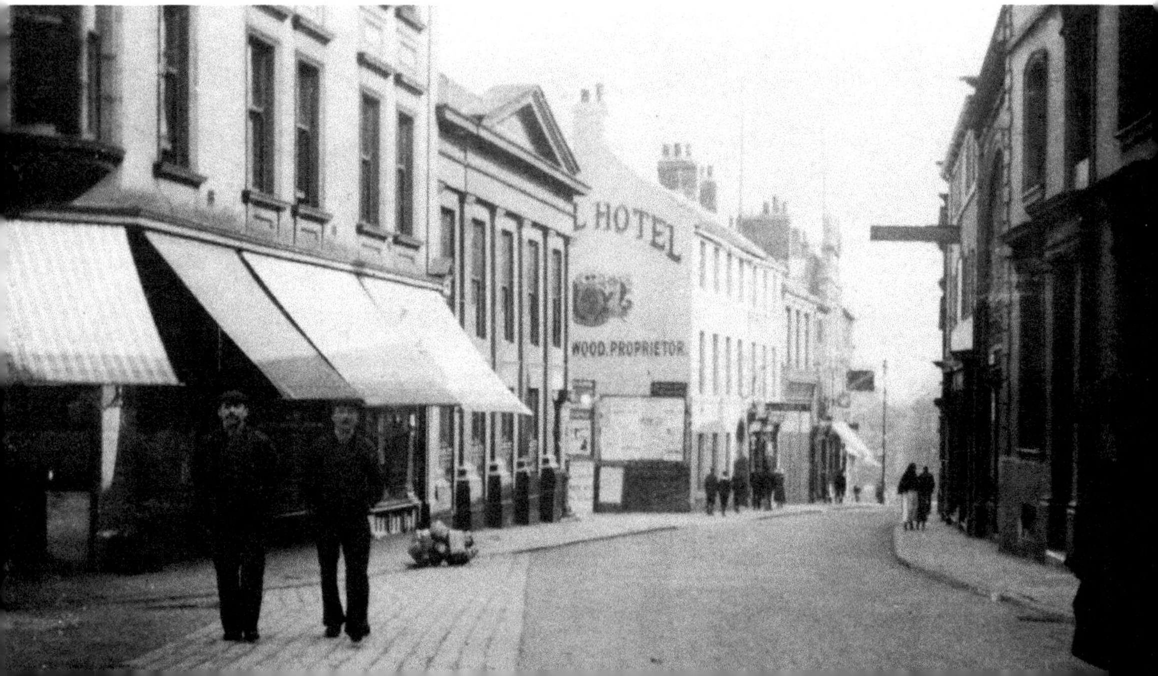

11. The Old No. 7

The Old No. 7 is a traditional, eighteenth-century, painted ashlar stone public house, which stands on Market Hill. It was praised by Ian Nairn as part of his 1972 *Across Britain* series of TV documentaries. Nairn was saddened that some potentially exciting spaces in Barnsley were unused. However, he highlights this as being the one exception. The round arched side entrance to the Old Bank Yard led to another Inn. The Temple of the Muses predated the Old No. 7, which was used by wine merchant H. Carter & Sons, as an ironmonger's shop and a printer's workshop. Antisocial behaviour meant locked metal gates were erected within the arched yard entrance in 2018.

At the turn of the last century Market Hill was a wide, cobbled space with market stalls all the way down one side, making this a bustling heart of the town. The Corn Exchange, which was built in 1824 on the corner with Shambles Street, dominated. This was destroyed by fire in 1927 and the stalls have been replaced with an austere car parking area where street signage and other clutter tend to dominate the views up Market Hill.

The Old No. 7, which was erected in 1715, had its number prominently displayed between two upper-floor windows. The number has now been replaced with the name of the current owners, and a new wooden porch was added at the entrance in 1996.

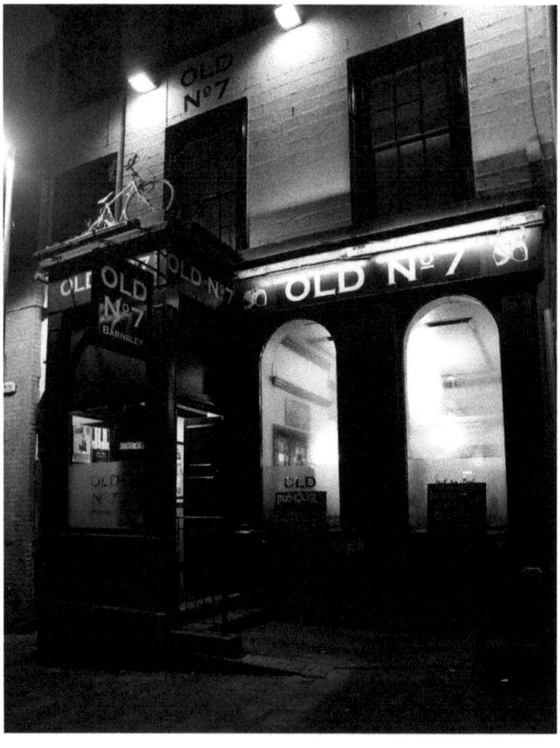

The wooden porch is a recent addition.

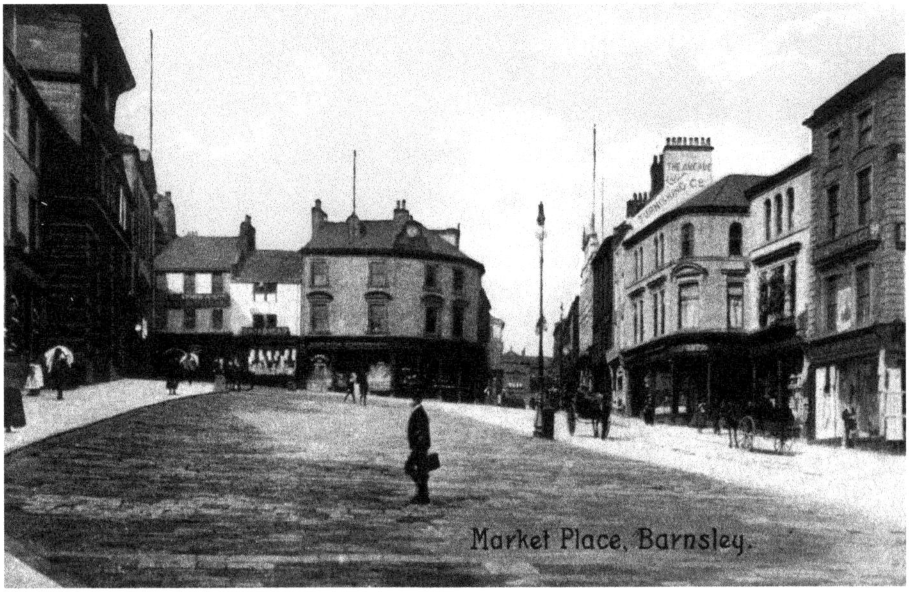

Market Hill in 1910. The Old No. 7 is next to the grand old Midland Bank.

The Old No. 7 could be regarded as a hidden gem given the adjacent modern bank building is set further forward and tends to dominate the much narrower frontage of the Old No. 7. There are also similarly unsympathetic modern structures on the other side. While the original Midland Bank building also projected, it was a much grander affair with arched windows and a decorative cornice. It was demolished in 1962.

The Old No. 7 is surprisingly large inside, and original arched cellars provide a basement level for functions. The Barnsley Sceptics meet here once a month. A guest speaker opens a discussion about a particular topic, ranging from cognitive dissonance to magic. One regular has painstakingly researched the pub's long history, which is on display in the bar in immaculate handwriting. The Old No. 7 is an authentic, locally brewed, real ale public house that would no doubt feature on any cultural tour of Barnsley town centre.

12. The Victorian Arcade and George Yard

These two historic yards close to the White Bear reflect the fine urban grain that typified the town prior to twentieth-century town centre redevelopment, when many of these medieval elements of the town were still visible. Some historic yards, such as Lancaster's Yard, have been lost completely. Burlington Arcade, which linked Eldon Street to May Day Green, had rows of shops along each side until 1973 when redevelopment created a blank side wall to Woolworths. It is now an unwelcoming back street.

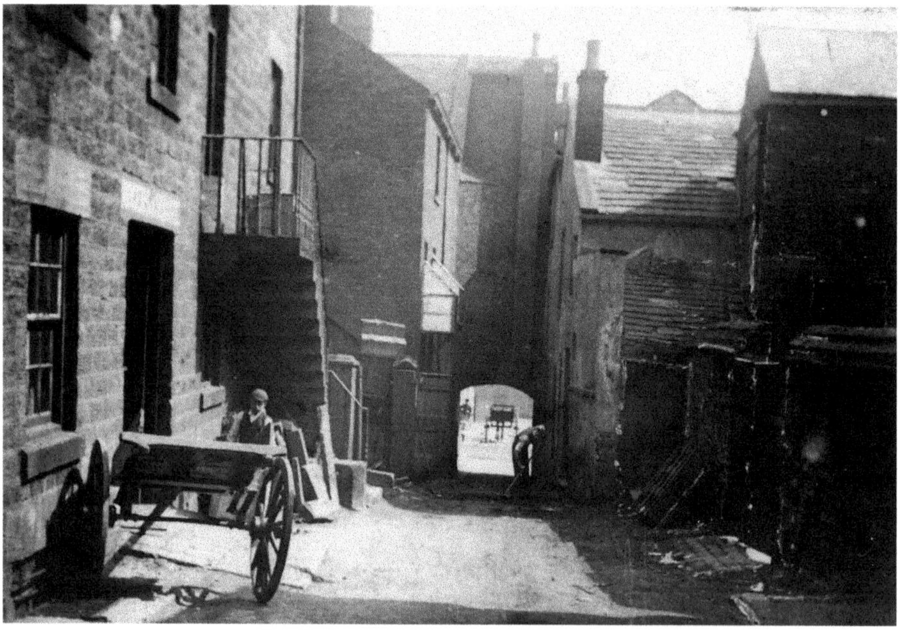

Lancaster Yard existed where the Town Hall is now located.

The Victorian Yard is a recent rebranding, as it was originally called Guest Yard and contained Broadgates Inn, built in 1667. Courts and yards served as unofficial trading points and meeting places. Fish was sold under the gateway on market days. The Market Hill entrance to the yard was created in 1892 and the yard was built to designs by local architects Wade & Turner. There are distinctive red columns made of cast iron, with the name of the foundry, Qualter and Smith Brothers and the date 1891. At the time of their installation the current Irish-

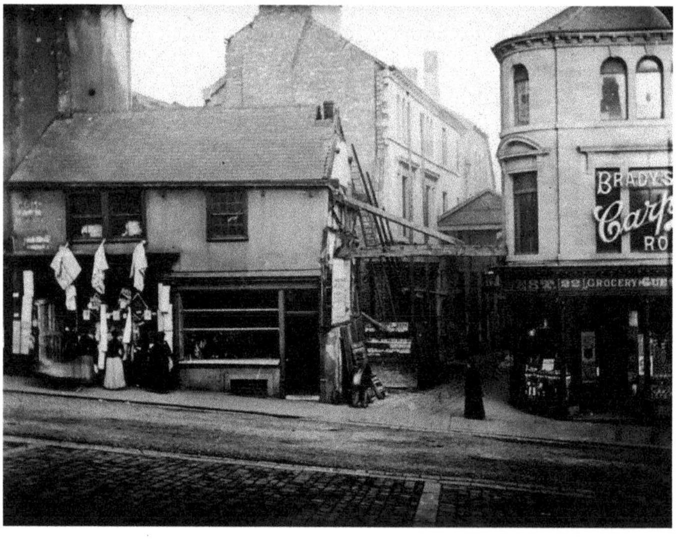

The entrance to the arcade was formed in 1893.

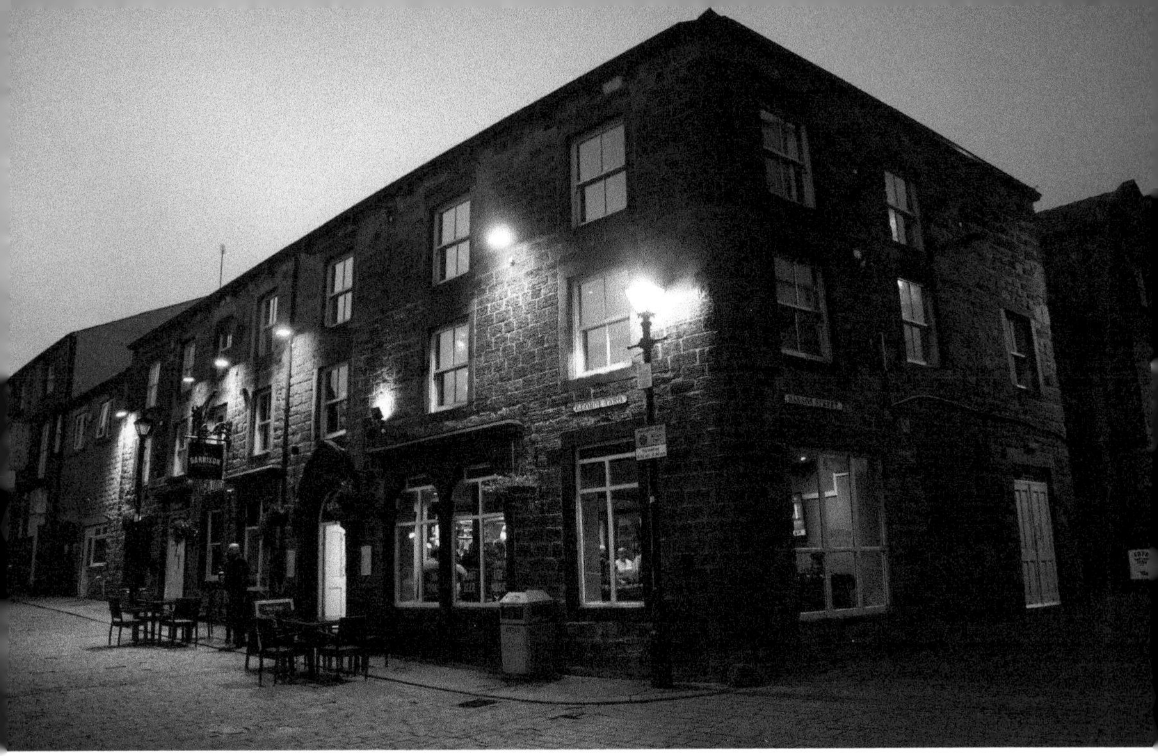

The Garrison public house in the refurbished George Yard.

themed pub was used by Guest Ltd, a high-end retailer selling, among other things, fine teas and coffees with a first-floor café. A butcher's shop bearing the name of Barnsley chop creator John Hirst was opposite.

George Yard was part of the same arcade company formed in 1890. It contained assembly rooms that held a wide variety of events, including musical recitals and art classes.[8] The yard also provided a route to the Public Hall. The George and Dragon Inn was a post-house with stabling for nearly fifty horses. Stones used to protect the adjacent building from damage are still in place. On market days there was a butter market.

The George Yard was pretty much derelict but has recently been restored. The Garrison public house was an old linen warehouse with a beehive carved above the stone in the arched doorway, together with the initials C. R. and the date 1873. The Beehive was also the name of a shop on Market Hill – one of the oldest boot and shoe shops in the Yorkshire area.

13. Cooper Gallery and Newman Bond Solicitors

During the reign of Charles II, Thomas Kersforth donated land and various buildings on Church Street that would lead to the formation of Barnsley Grammar School. While the current building dates from 1769, a new schoolroom was initially erected in 1665. Further extensions in 1784 and 1874 allowed for a Sunday school. Meanwhile, in 1546 the Archbishop of York, Robert Holgate, had established a

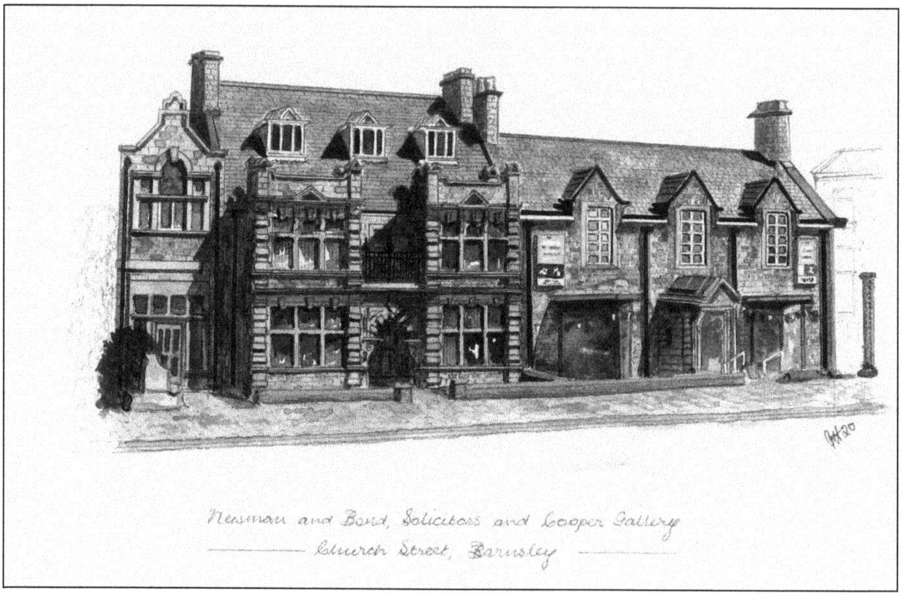

The best view is obtained from St Mary's churchyard.

school at Hemsworth. In 1887, the Holgate Grammar School amalgamated with Barnsley Grammar School, which changed its name to the Holgate School.

Initially having around 100 students, increased pupil numbers meant that the Holgate School sought new premises around a kilometre away on Shaw Lane. Opened in 1912, this new school was attended by Michael Parkinson and

The Cooper Gallery has a peaceful garden area containing art installations.

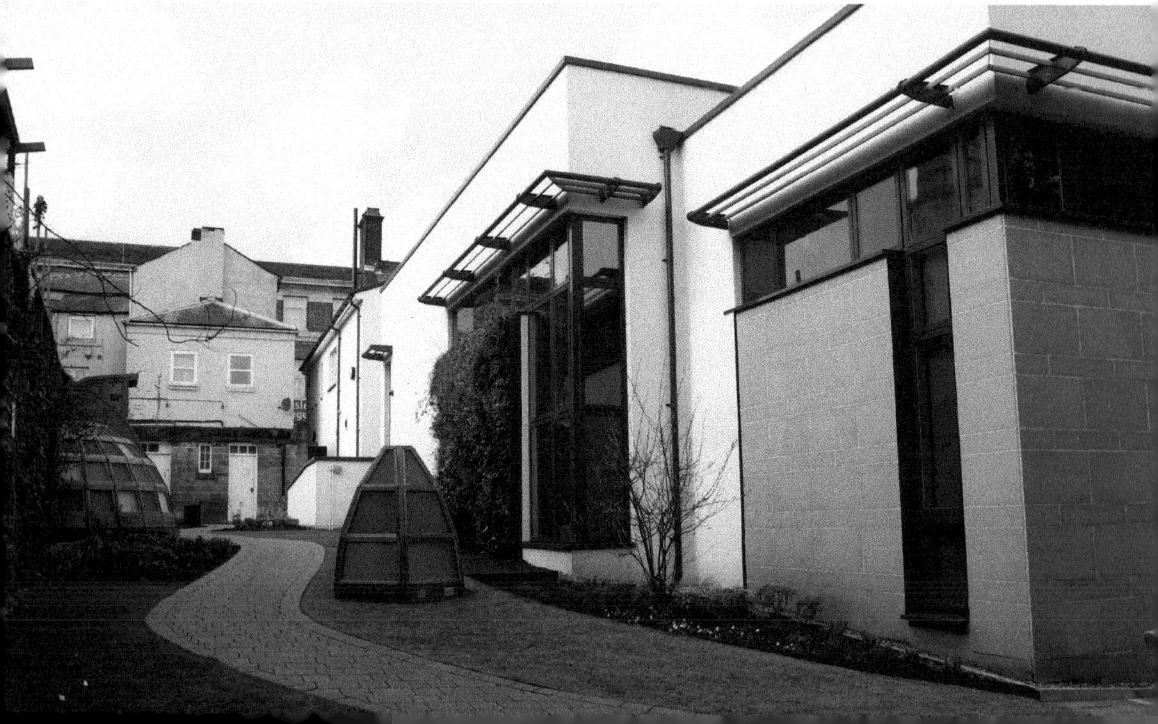

Stan Richards among others. The school closed in 2012 and despite efforts to have the building listed, this fine building was demolished to accommodate the staff car park for Horizon Academy (the home of world-renowned Barnsley Youth Choir).

Samuel Cooper, who had inherited a fortune from his father (a coal, iron and linen magnate) bought the Church Street building in 1912. Born in 1831, Samuel was baptised in St Mary's Church, on the opposite side of Church Street. On his travels around Europe Samuel collected hundreds of paintings and drawings.

Childless, Samuel Cooper left this building and his art collection in trust, for use as an art gallery. As well as the gallery, he provided money for a mining disaster monument at Kendray and for the Beckett Hospital. Sir Michael Sadler donated some works by J. M. W. Turner and wine and spirit merchant Thomas Fox (1860–1956) gave money for the building of the Fox Wing (built in 1934). Modern projecting glass bays were added at the front, and more recently two modern galleries have been added at the rear. At this time the main public entrance to the building was reinstated through the attractive central Edwardian porch.

In November 2019, Arts Council funding allowed the refurbishment of the Cooper Gallery Cottage at the rear of the gallery into a modern artist studio space, with exhibition areas and a café. This is accessed from the alteration of a window to a door on Eastgate.

14. The Lamproom Theatre and Pinfold Steps

The family and friends of James and Elizabeth Taylor, the founders of the first Methodist Society in Barnsley, built and opened the former Wesleyan Chapel in 1794 on what was called Pinfold Hill. This is one of the places in Barnsley where John Wesley is said to have preached.

The Taylors' eldest son, John, was a reed maker in the local linen industry. Hope Works, which was built around 1820, was next to the Chapel. Linen weaving was at this time the principal industry in Barnsley. While the Hope Works dominated the lower side of Sackville Street, it followed the topography, so the chapel was itself the most imposing feature on Pinfold Hill. However, it now has to compete with modern incursions that have transformed the skyline.

This Grade II listed building remained a chapel until 1948, when it became the base for Barnsley Boys' Club. Money was donated by the Miners' Welfare Committee to help establish the Boys' Club, which opened in January 1933 in a school on Baker Street. It quickly relocated to Nelson Street, and it was here that the Prince of Wales visited the Boys' Club in 1933.

In 1998, the Boys' Club building was purchased for use as a theatre with funds initially raised by the Theatre Royal appeal. The Lamproom Theatre has clear links with the mining industry as forty original miners' lamps have been installed in the auditorium. Each lamp represents a different Barnsley colliery.

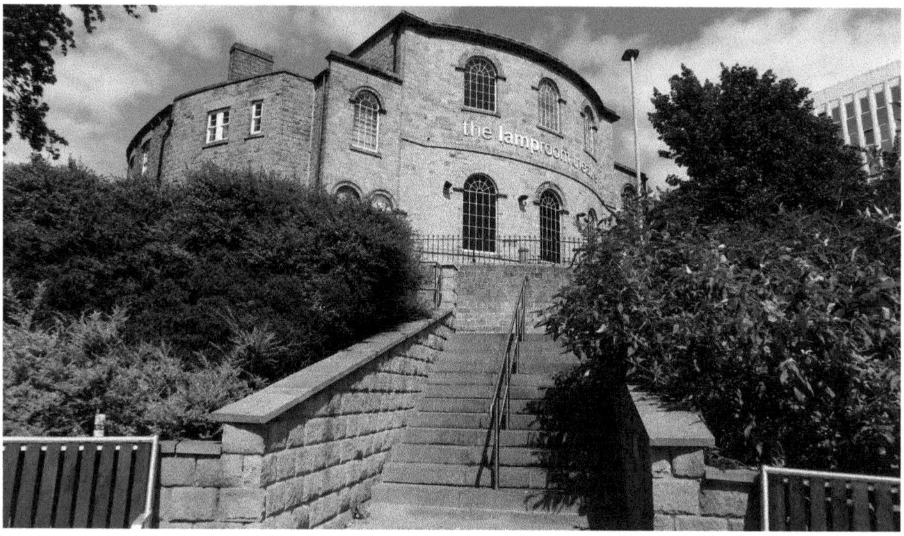

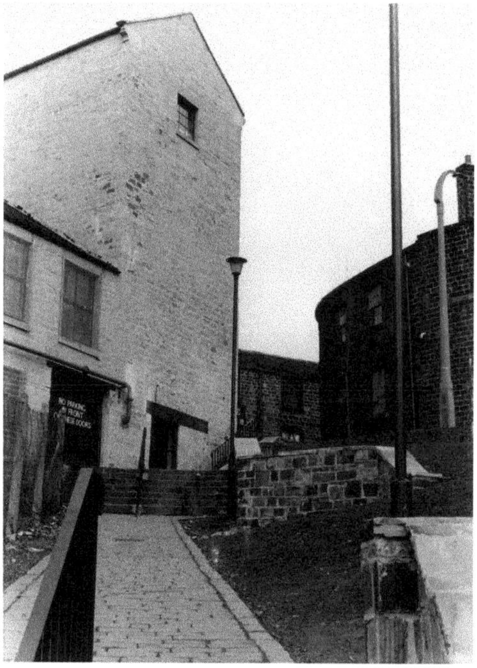

Above: The theatre opened up again on 21 May 2021 after the easing of Covid-19 restrictions.

Left: Looking up the Pinfold Steps prior to the demolition of Hope Mill.

The Lamproom Theatre is at the top of Pinfold Steps, which are a significant feature from the town's agricultural past. The Pinfold was used by local police to keep stray animals and was positioned on a level piece of ground near the steps. Drovers brought their cattle and sheep from the town end via Shambles Street, which was then known as Westgate. Every Monday cattle markets were held at Kendray Street, and there were many smaller slaughterhouses and butchers' stalls in the Market Place.

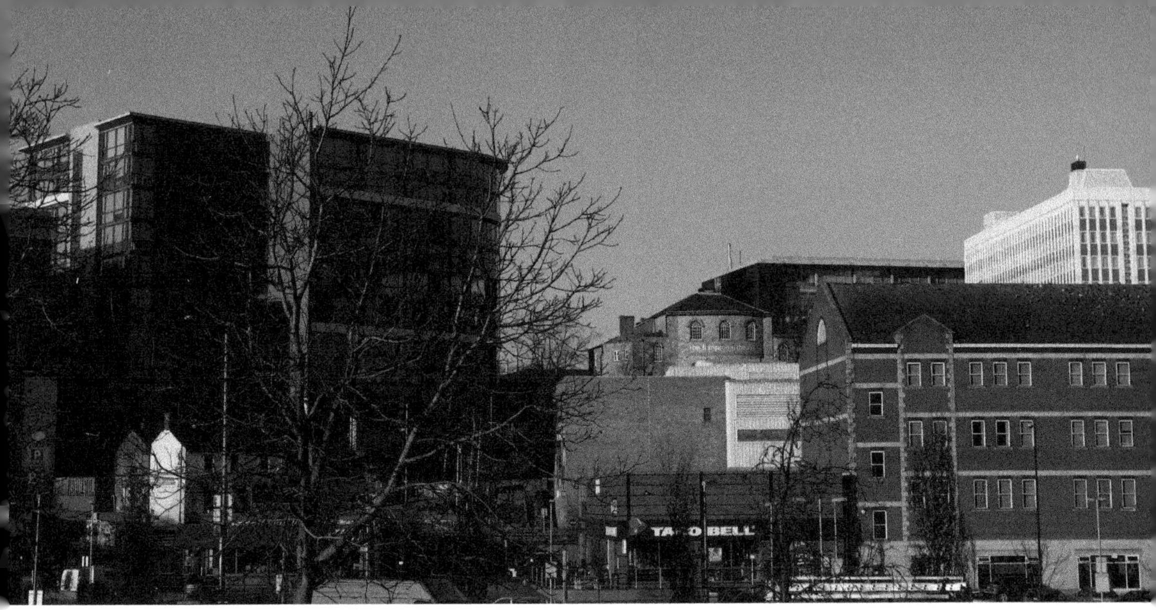

Large modern developments have tended to dwarf this listed building.

15. Wesleyan Methodist Association Chapel

At various locations around the town red plaques form the James Hudson Taylor trail, including one on this chapel built on Blucher Street in 1829. James Taylor, the founder of the Wesleyan Chapel at Pinfold Hill, was the great grandfather of James Hudson Taylor, a renowned missionary who first went to China in 1853 at the age of twenty-one. James Hudson Taylor, who had studied Mandarin and medicine, attended many meetings in this chapel. In 1865, he founded the China Inland Mission, which sent hundreds of missionaries to East Asia. Two Sunday school teachers from the chapel, joined him at the China Inland Mission.

During the Boxer Rebellion of 1900 many of these missionaries and some of their children were killed. After some personal tragedies of his own Hudson Taylor died in 1905. Another James Hudson Taylor trail red plaque is opposite here: on the Salem Wesleyan Reform Chapel, built in 1825.

In 1958, the chapel was acquired by the Barnsley British Co-operative Society who used it for a social club. The original church organ was removed and a new floor introduced. In 1982, it became a religious building once again when the Hope House Church and Christian School opened.

The gable and Palladian arch windows of the original chapel front can be seen above the flat parapet roof of the new rusticated ashlar stone front, which was added in 1901.

The original chapel was built by Barnsley-born architect, town planner and Sunday school teacher John Whitworth, who was also responsible for the enlargement of the Lamproom Theatre, when wings were added in 1810.

John Whitworth had a strong influence on the appearance of Barnsley as much of the old town was rebuilt, with new streets created and many new buildings erected.

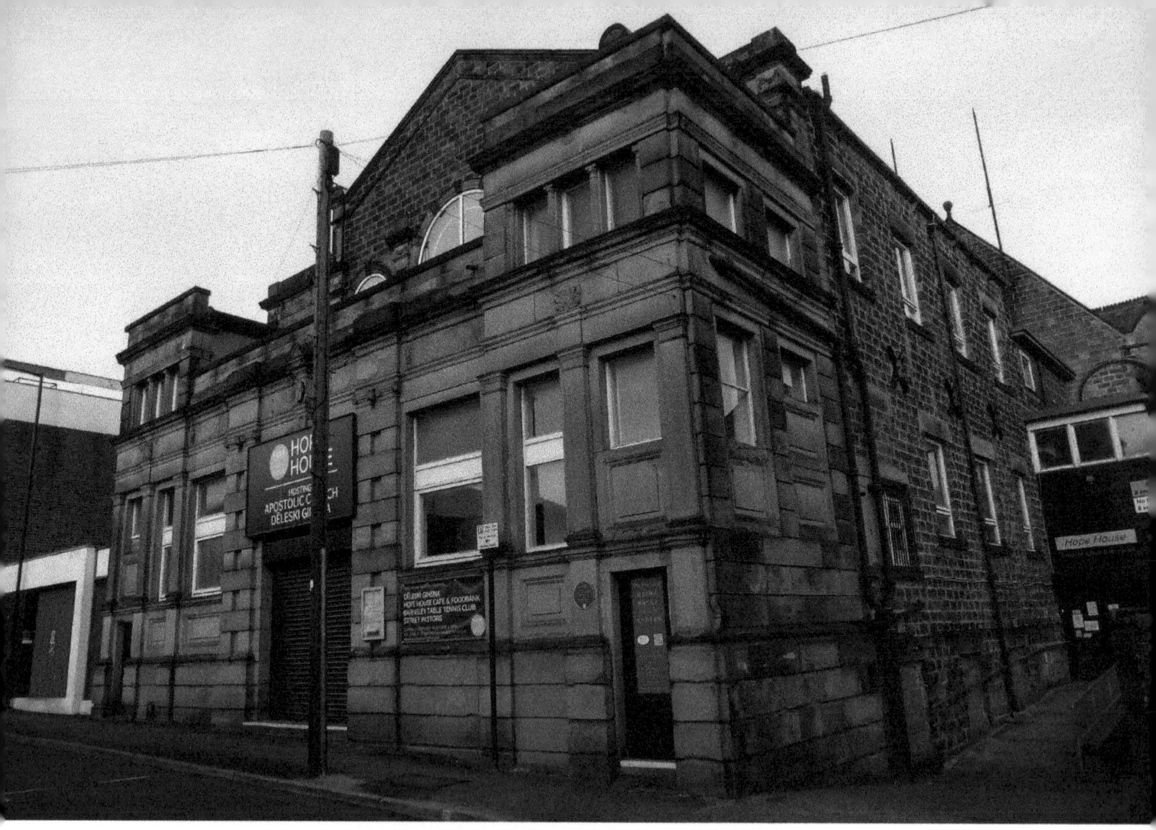

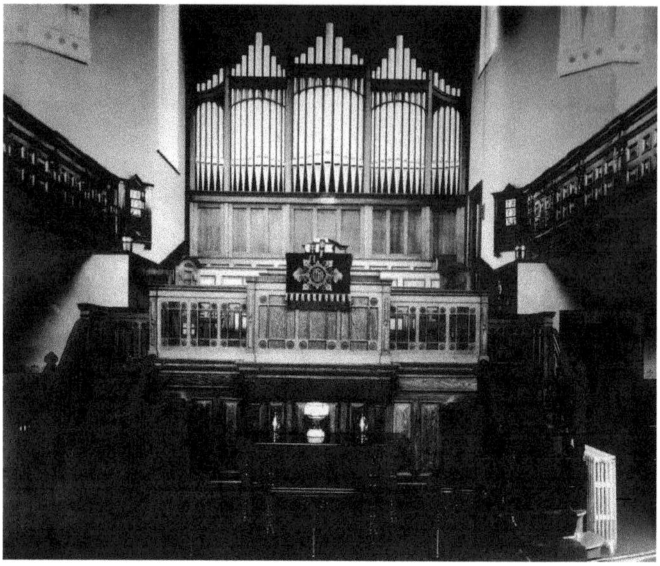

Above: The ashlar stone front is a later addition.

Left: The organ installed in 1928 was removed when the Cooperative inserted a floor.

He was born in 1779 and died at the age of eighty-four in 1863. Unfortunately, many of the notable buildings he designed or helped to design have perished. These include the first Sunday school in Barnsley at Churchfields; School Street was named after this building. Other lost structures attributed to John Whitworth were the Barnsley Obelisk, the Old Corn Exchange and Market House. He also assisted the architect of the Congregational Church on Regent Street.

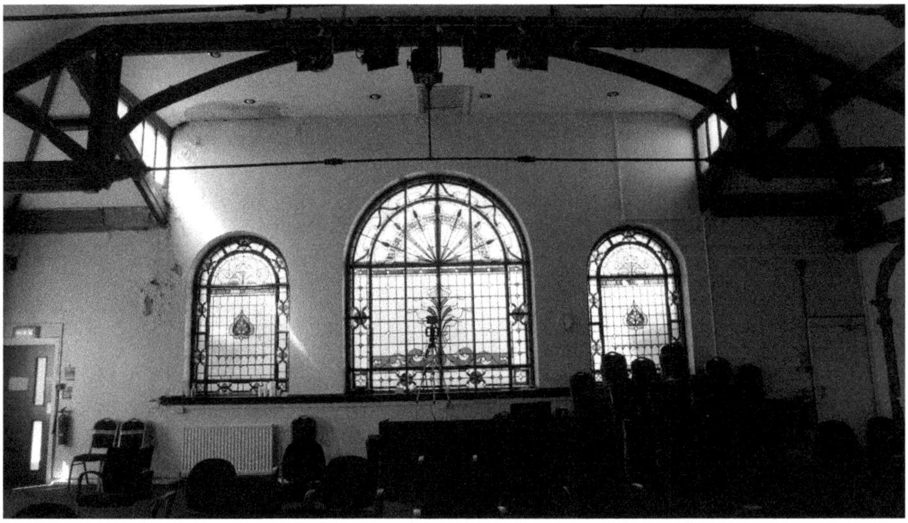

The upper floor is now a used by the Latvian Church.

16. Temperance Hall

Purchased by the Temperance Society in 1880, this building was originally built for the Oddfellows, a fraternal organisation similar to the Freemasons. Local architect W. J. Hindle based his design on a classical Ionic plan – typically a simple rectangle with precise symmetry. It was this uniformity that gave these temples their beauty. Built in the year Queen Victoria was crowned (1837), the hall has two Ionic columns and four pilasters supporting a simple entablature and pediment. The arrangement of columns and pilasters suggest a classical form known as *dystile* (two columns) in *antis*. The side walls of the temple project forward and terminate with a corner pilaster or *antas*.

Since it was built the use of the building has changed many times, first being a furniture warehouse in 1850. In 1909, it became a private school and was renamed The Atheneum – a very grand term used in the names of important libraries or institutions for literary or scientific study. It was then less ostentatiously named the Cosy Picture House (1923–28) before it became the Central School of Dancing, reverting back to a warehouse in 1952. More controversially for a Temperance Society building, it has also been a pub called Panama Joes.[9]

The Temperance Hall is one of the last remaining buildings on Pitt Street mentioned by Niklaus Pevsner. Pitt Street was where many eminent local people lived, including John Whitworth and James Hudson Taylor. Pevsner extolled the virtues of the neighbouring Weslyan Chapel, designed by James Simpson and built in 1846. He singled out the elegant Ellis Free School from 1831, located on the opposite corner, as being particularly fine. Another glowing reference is made to the scholarly and thoughtful design by Rickman of St George Church, built in 1821, which had some excellent stained glass by Allen. Pevsner concludes with St George's Place, an attractive Georgian Terrace.

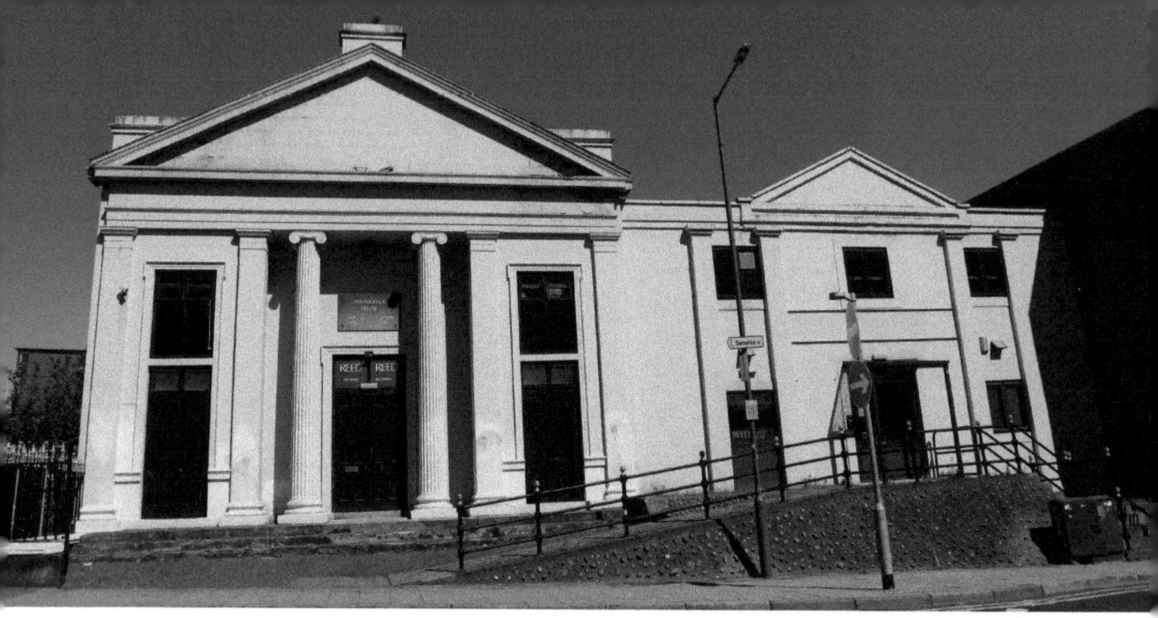

A recent extension disrupts the classical rectangular form of a classical Ionic building.

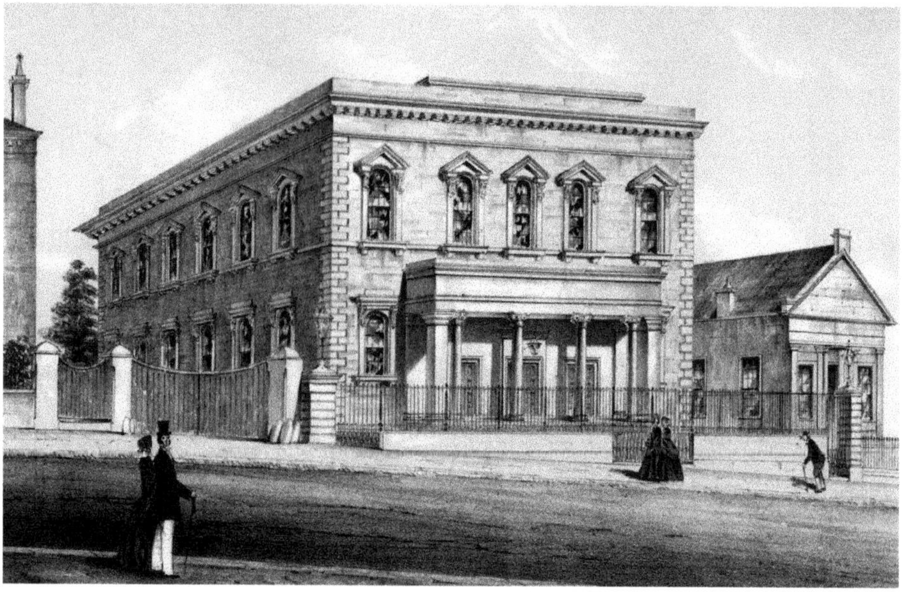

The Wesleyan Chapel, Pitt Street, dwarfed the Temperance Hall in 1890.

Pevsner said Pitt Street was the finest street in Barnsley and there are still strong indications in the area around Holy Rood Roman Catholic Church of the character before these demolitions. The loss of the Ellis Free School was also lamented by Ian Nairn in his documentary on Barnsley, but he muses at least the replacement YMCA building has been designed by a local architect with a good reputation. This was John Poulson. In 1974, Poulson was jailed for corruption and bribery in what was a national scandal implicating several MPs, police officers, civil servants and health authority officials.

17. Former Coach and Horses and Peel Square North

The Sough Dyke, which supplied the many linen mills in this part of the town, passed through Peel Square. The dyke passed under the Packhorse Bridge at the bottom of Market Hill and there was a row of shops in the middle of Peel Square. South of the shops was known as Peashill Nook and the north was called Sough Bridge. Dog Lane, an ancient footway from the Shambles, crossed the Sough Dyke and exists today as an alternative route to Peel Square.[10]

Three linked Italianate listed buildings form a mostly unaltered ashlar stone terrace on the north side of Peel Square. Built in 1857, they display the same spandrel detailing around the arched first-floor windows. Before becoming a bank in 1912 the corner of the terrace was the Coach and Horses public house. Now Virgin Money, the building extends along Market Hill and has a rounded corner bay surmounted by a cupola. There is a lead-covered lantern with swept sides and elliptical lights. This building, and in particular the cupola, are dominant features when approaching Peel Square either via Eldon Street, Queen Street or Market Street.

Originally the Market Hill elevation, which contained Reynolds and Wadworth's Ironmongers, recessed then extended over a yard entrance, with a

Market stalls add colour, although the council feel that they detract from the listed building.

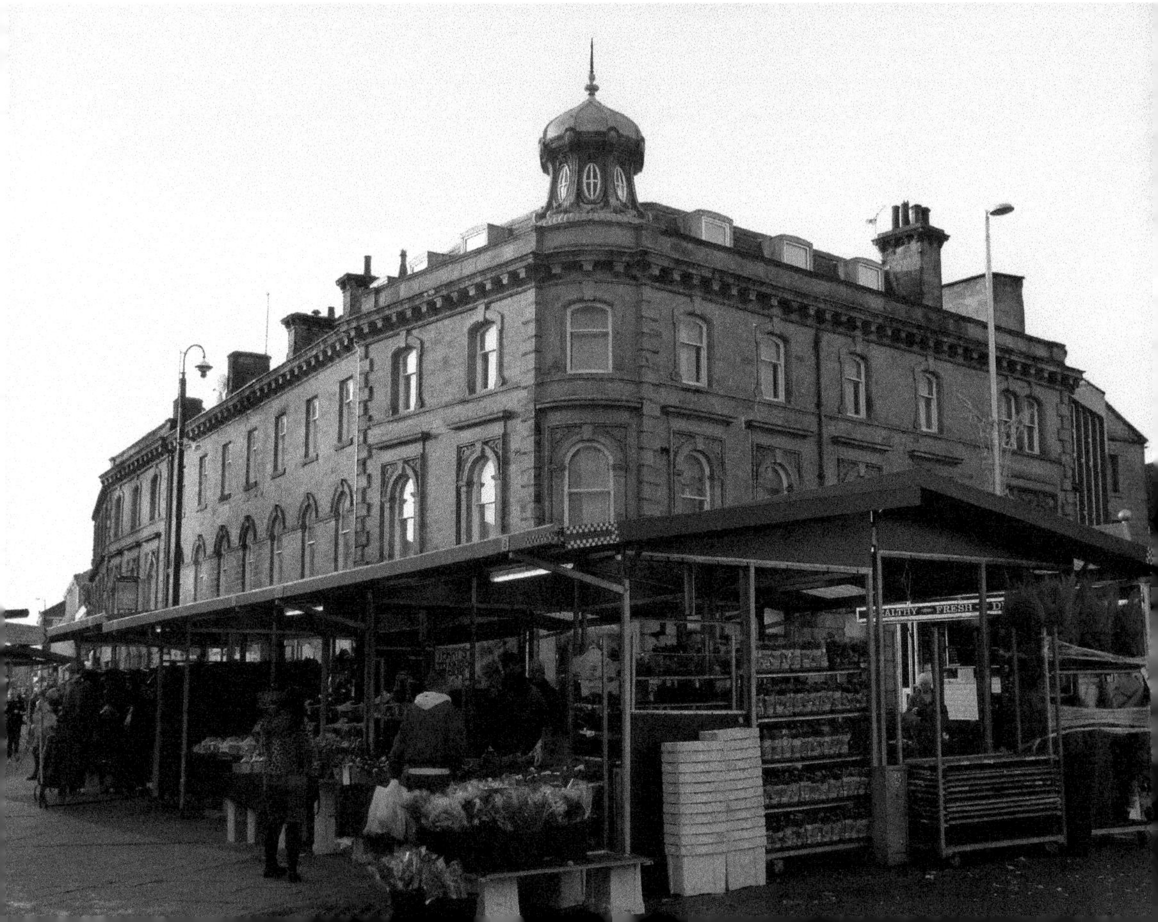

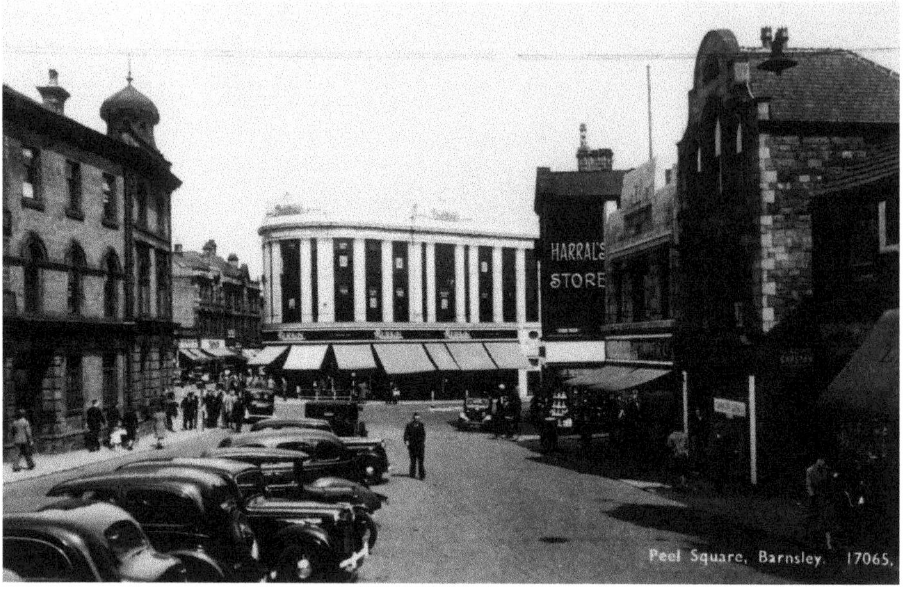

Peel Square in 1935, with cars dominating the space.

fine shop with a pedimented gable on the other side. This attractive element of the street scene looking down Market Hill was lost by demolition and infilling with the modern Lloyds Bank building. While high-quality materials are used, the new bank appears shoehorned into too small a gap. The excessive height of the black granite and glazed frontage dominates the dignified cornice and parapet on the Coach and Horses.

Peel Square has a number of connections to other streets and yards, but in the days of horse-drawn transport it was open and spacious. It then became completely dominated by traffic, being both a main route to the M1 and a car park. It was pedestrianised in 1992 and permanent market stalls were added. As these stalls have recently been removed it would be nice to think that in the future these would once again extend up Market Hill.

18. The Chronicle Building and Peel Square South and East

The *Barnsley Chronicle* was first published on 16 October 1858, when it was printed at Matchett's Yard on Queen Street. Local papers record the social history of a town and while many local newspapers were established, they were often short-lived. The paper's co-founder, Thomas Lingard, who had supported the Chartist movement, was the driving force behind building the new premises in 1877. Peel Square was the at the centre of local events and crowds would gather in front of the Chronicle Buildings. One owner was Captain Bruce Vernon Wentworth – MP, cricketer and the last family member to own Wentworth Castle. He sold it to Sir Joseph Hewitt who helped form the Barnsley Pals.[11]

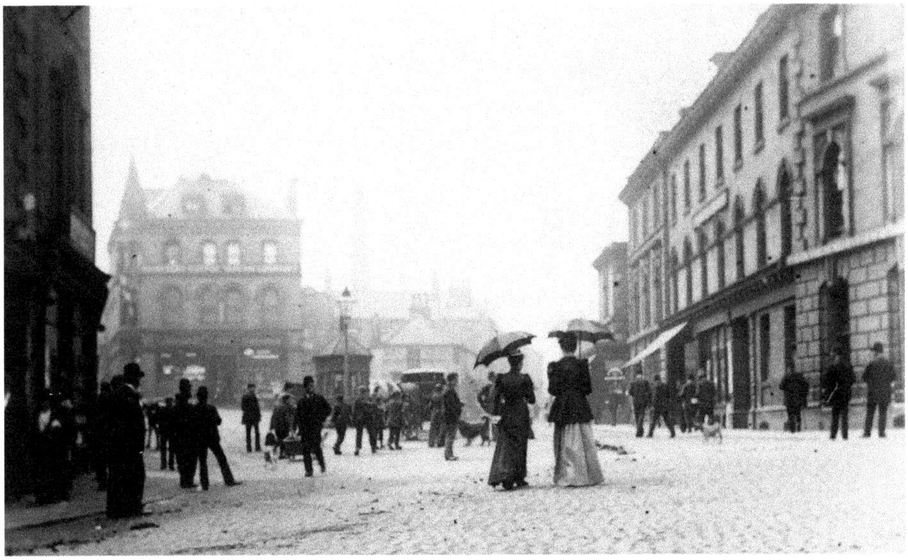

In 1890, the building that catches the eye is the former Chronicle Building.

The Barnsley Coffee Tavern Company occupied the upper floors and when the *Barnsley Chronicle* moved to new premises on Eastgate the ground floor was primarily used for banking. In 1994, Tetley took over the building and, after a competition in the *Barnsley Chronicle*, called it Tommy Wallocks. This was a derivation of a name associated with various local characters who lived in the town.

In Peel Square there are three pubs on a narrow crossroads: The Corner Pin, Chennell's Bar and the Chronicle Building, now called Chambers Bar. However, the Imperial Hotel, would have made four. The Imperial Hotel was a superbly

Peel Square as it is today, with remodelling to remove market stalls underway.

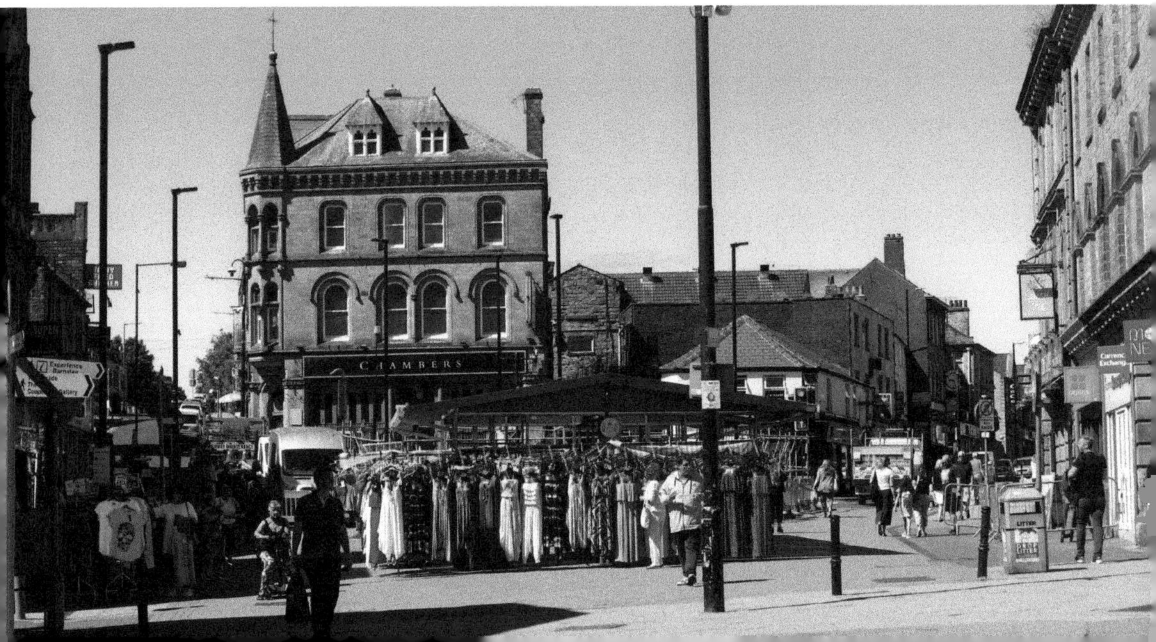

detailed stone building that dominated the south side of the square. It was demolished in the late 1950s to be replaced by utilitarian concrete shops of little architectural merit. Whatever the merits of the case for demolition, Peel Square should not have had such a drab replacement foisted upon it.

In front of the Chronicle Building are decorative wrought-iron entrance arches to disused male and female Edwardian subterranean public toilets. In other towns, such as Berwick and Seaburn, similar examples have obtained listed building status due to their significant contribution to social history. Furthermore, among other things, Stainborough-born Joseph Bramah patented an improved toilet design in 1778 and his name is given to the nearby Wetherspoons. Sadly, this turn-of-the-century landmark is currently being removed along with all of the market stalls.

19. The Courthouse

With some notable exceptions, Regent Street has retained most of its historic buildings and could be claimed to be the finest street in Barnsley. This ashlar stone Italianate-style building was designed by Charles Reeves, the government architect for county courts, and has the royal coat of arms over the main entrance. There are prominent decorated masonry blocks and quoins with irregular shallow channels or vermiculation. At first-floor level there are round-arched windows with elongated keystones and spandrels applied to the stonework between each arch. The prominent bracketed cornice is supported by Corinthian scroll consoles.

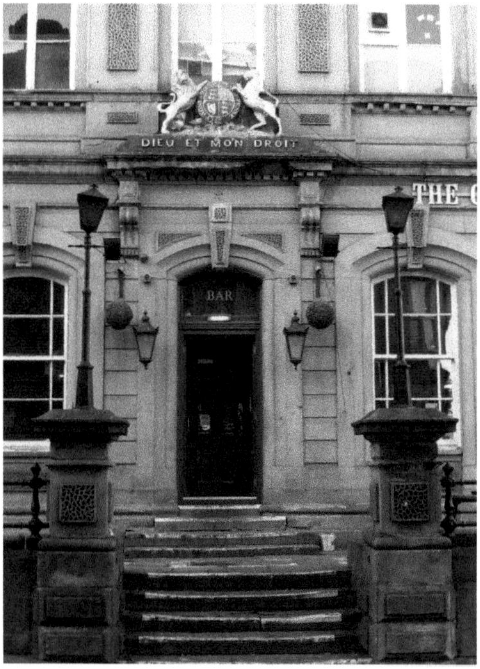

The coat of arms over the entrance reveals the original use.

Built as Barnsley's courthouse in 1861, this elaborately detailed building is highly significant in Barnsley's development from a small market town to a prosperous industrial one because it opened up the town to the railway revolution. Barnsley already had the Exchange station, built twenty years earlier, but this had a single platform and limited links. Barnsley's main station on the North Midlands Railway line was located at Cudworth.

In the early days of railways George Stephenson only put down railway lines in areas where the gradients were not too difficult. This is why Cudworth station served Barnsley, and whoever wished to get to Cudworth had to use the horse-bus leaving from the Royal Hotel.

The existing courthouse was converted to provide a ticket office, waiting rooms and staff quarters and the adjacent goods yard was formed to serve a two-coach, pull-and-push shuttle train called the *Cudworth Flyer*. The courthouse became known as the Top station due to its elevated position and was used to connect Barnsley to main-line services until 1958.

The station opened to passenger traffic in 1870 and the *Cudworth Flyer* passed over the Oaks Viaduct. This 331-metre-long viaduct spanned the Dearne Valley at Hoyle Mill and carried the Midland Railways Cudworth to Barnsley line. It was deemed unsafe in 1965 and was demolished in 1968. It was thought at the time to be Britain's largest railway bridge.

In the town centre a bridge crossed Eldon Street and there was also a viaduct through the town for services from Sheffield and the Penistone–Barnsley–Doncaster service. When the Court House station closed the top of the viaduct was covered in grass like a green flyover. The arches were all blocked up apart from one left open to access the bus station.

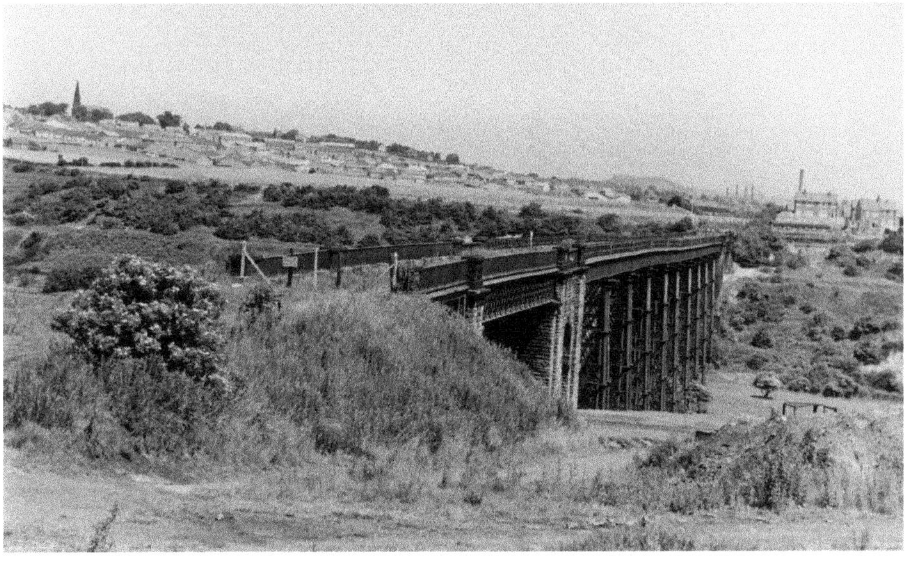

The Oaks Viaduct just prior to demolition in 1968.

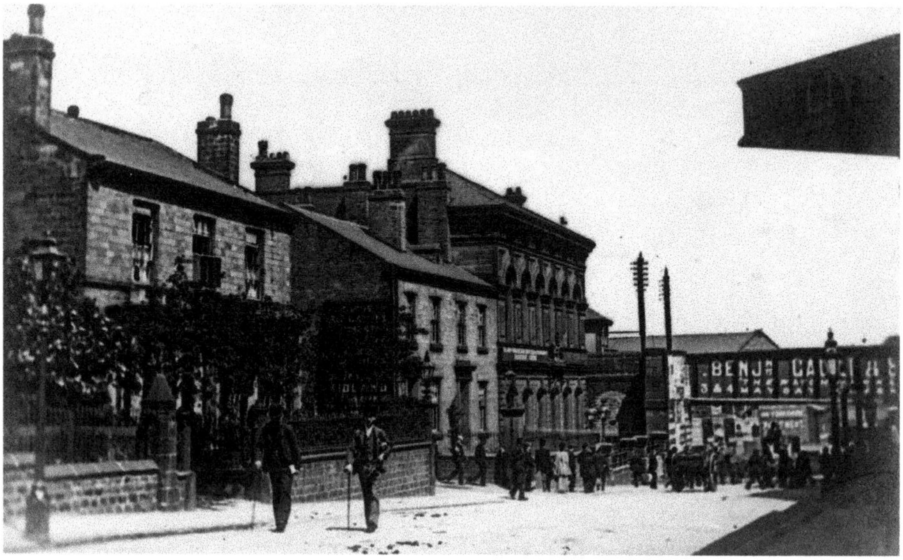

The Courthouse station required a bridge over Regent Street as seen in 1910.

20. New Courthouse

Within just nine years of building a courthouse on Regent Street a second was opened in 1871. The new High Renaissance-style courthouse with registrar, bankruptcy and bailiff's offices was mostly paid for by the Midland Railway. It was designed by Thomas Charles Sorby, a London-based architect who emigrated to Canada.[12] In 1890, a similar Sorby-designed courthouse was built on Hastings Street, Vancouver.[13]

There are steps up to the grand Regent Street entrance. This is set to one side within a Doric portico, which has a decorated entablature supporting a parapet containing a cartouche. The rusticated Gibbs surrounds on the square arch ground-floor windows are employed to give the impression of strength and solidity. This classical approach is named after James Gibbs, a leading Anglo-Palladian architect who designed St Martin-in-the-Fields in London. The large ashlar stone blocks with their deep channelled joints visually support the more delicate first-floor Ionic colonnade with five round-arched windows and balustrades.

Pevsner described the ashlar-faced *cinquecento* county court as being dignified, but also a little aloof. The local press heralded it as unquestionably the most handsome building on Regent Street.

The building is now in office use, and it has been much altered internally. However, the first-floor courtroom still exists, albeit partitioned to accommodate BIADS Barnsley Dementia Support Group. On Eastgate a separate side door and staircase was needed for the courthouse keeper's residence, which now leads to the courtroom.

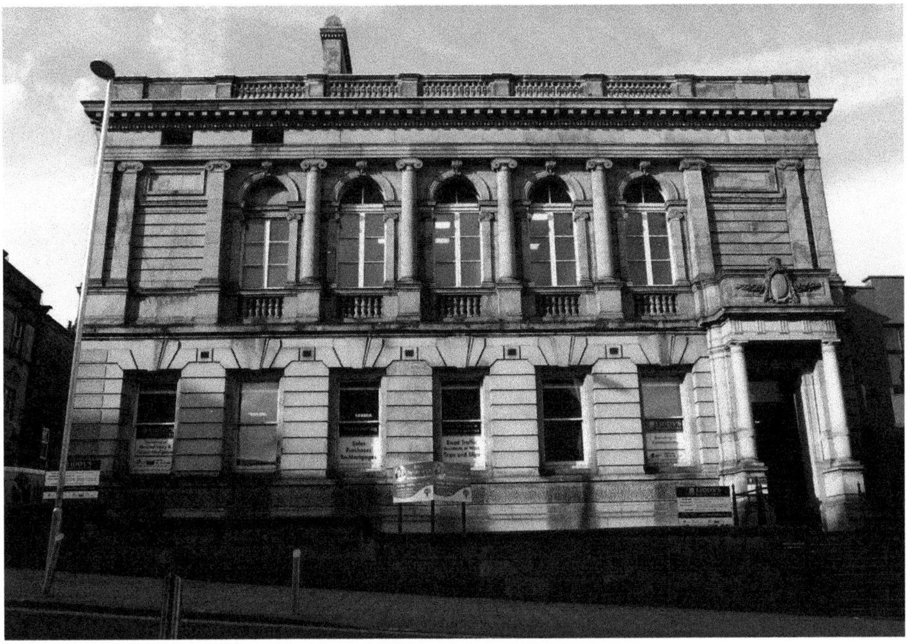

The Borough Courthouse on Westgate was built in 1878.

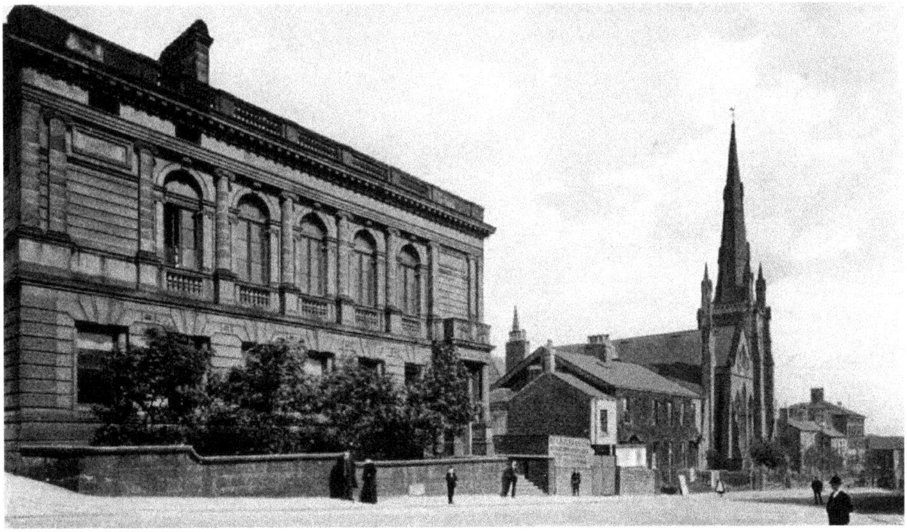

The Congregational Church dominated Regent Street prior to its demolition in 1971.

The building is one of an impressive group of historic buildings located around the corner of Eastgate and Regent Street. When it was built, the Congregational Church, with its tall spire, was a dominant feature in the town's skyline. It was located between the new and former courthouses. These acted as bookends with the church and some private houses between.

The Congregational church has gone, replaced by a boxy office block. However, this has a blue plaque for Matthew Carrington Sykes (1852–1922), a local philanthropist. The Barnsley Civic Trust has promoted many blue plaques around the town, including for local comedians Harry Worth and Charlie Williams.

21. The Queens Hotel

Occupying a prime location, at the bottom of Regent Street, this was Barnsley's grandest Victorian hotel, club, wine and temperance bar. The former Queens Hotel was ideally located between the town's two railway stations and the bus station. This very grand building was erected in 1874 and designed by local architects Wade and Turner, who also designed the NUM headquarters building in the same year.

On the corner of Eldon Street and Regent Street this Grade II listed building is a classical style three-storey building with an attic level behind a parapet wall. There is a symmetrical façade to each street frontage with round-arched, ground-floor windows incorporating carved-head keystones in sets of three. The carved keystones are a mixture of lions, eagles and royal heads.

The grand main entrance onto Regent Street is in the form of a triumphal arch, a popular motif based on the Arch of Constantine I in Rome. The arched entrance has a carved head of Queen Victoria as the keystone. There is a stone cornice and decorative balconette between two capitals, supporting stone flower pots. The vertical balusters, a name derived from the shape of the pomegranate flower, are also seen in the parapet, which sits on a bracketed cornice supported by consoles.

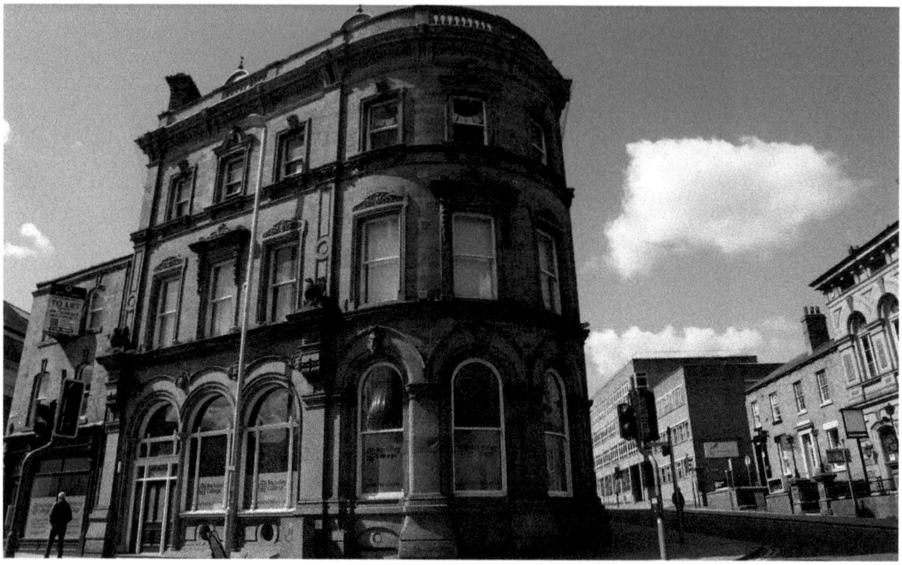

The impressively adorned former Queens Hotel immediately meets the visitor's eye when leaving the Transport Interchange.

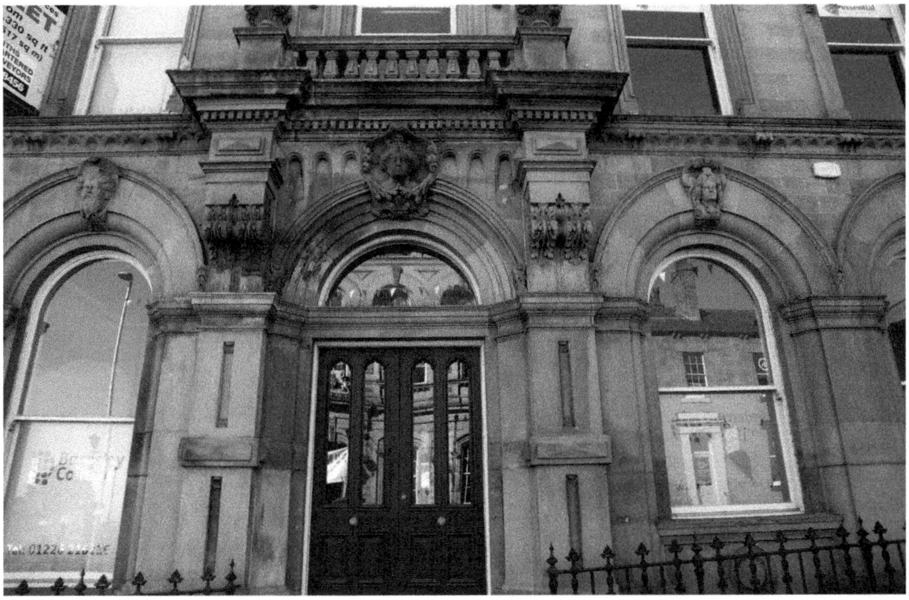

Leeds-based sculptor Benjamin Payler provided the carved stonework, which includes a bust of Queen Victoria over the Regent Street entrance.

The bridge serving Court House station cut across the bottom of Regent Street. Clearly this would have had a seriously negative impact on this fine building. The activity from the bus and two railway stations meant traffic at this corner was hectic. In the days of steam trains and before unleaded petrol and catalytic converters, air quality indicators would have been off the scale. The hotel was blackened by soot, but the aesthetic rewards of cleaning can put the building

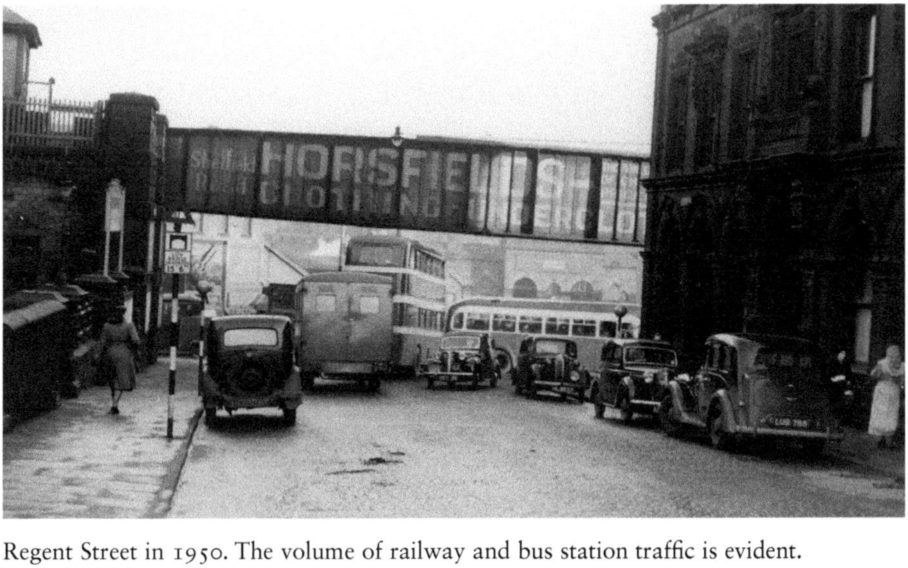

Regent Street in 1950. The volume of railway and bus station traffic is evident.

fabric at risk by choosing the wrong cleaning method. Sandstone buildings are not homogeneous as portions can have different mineral content and there is potential for damage to the stonemason Benjamin Payler's outstanding workmanship. It is a testament to those responsible for the cleaning that these and other intricate details such as the stone eagles have been preserved.

Briefly called the Clarence Hotel there was a gentlemen's bar in the late 1950s and early 1960s.[14] The Queens Hotel changed hands many times but finally closed in 1972 and the premises were renovated, and it is now the Queens Court Business Centre.

22. Locke Park Columns

On the edge of Barnsley town centre, the superbly laid out People's Park was dedicated to the memory of railway engineer Joseph Locke and donated to the town by his widow Phoebe. It officially opened on 10 June 1862. However, when Phoebe Locke died Sarah McCreery donated further land in the memory of her sister and it now comprises 47 acres of parkland which links directly to the open countryside to the south of Racecommon Lane, an old route indicated on the Ordnance Survey map of 1855. In addition to the outstanding flora and fauna of the park it contains four of my fifty buildings.

The Locke Park Pavilion Tea Rooms, which opened in 1911, are an important feature, as are the drinking fountain from Peel Square and the gatehouses at the entrances but a very unexpected and somewhat ironic feature are four classical

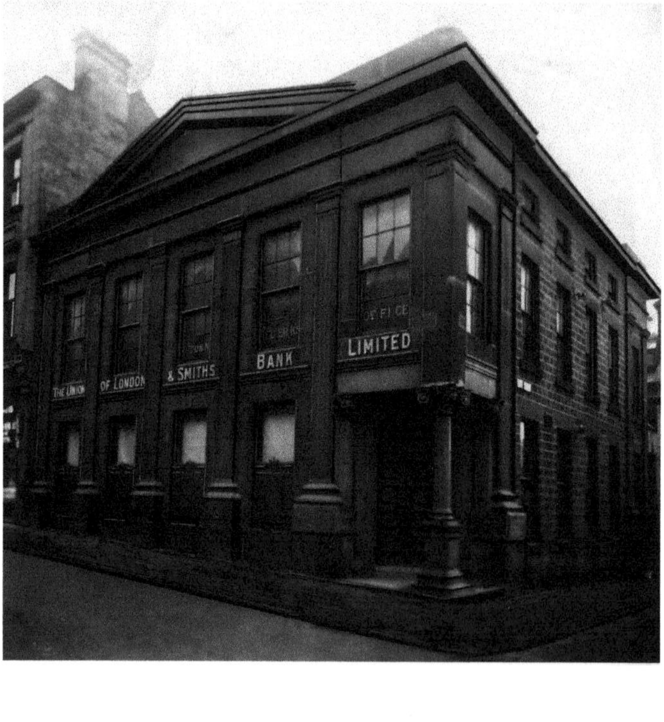

The columns were removed from the Union of London and Smiths Bank.

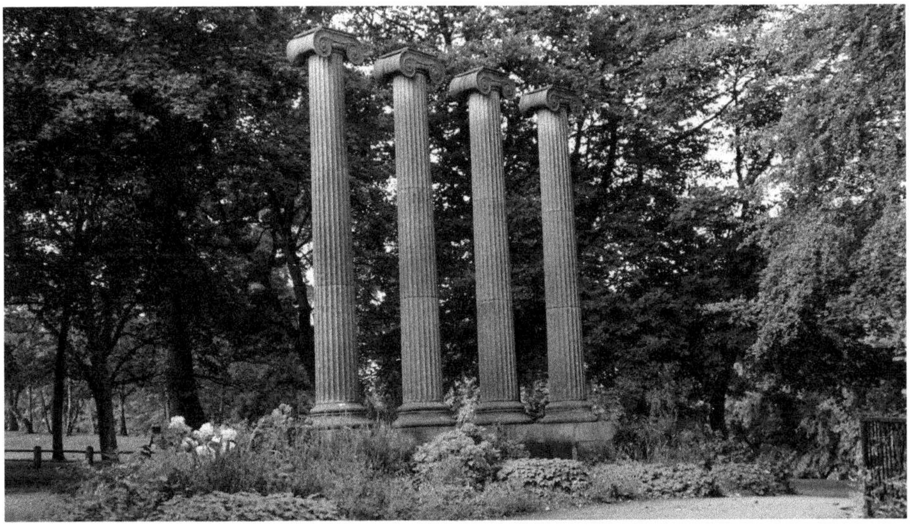

The Ionic columns are often incorrectly referred to locally as the Corinthian columns.

Ionic columns. These columns were originally the grand portico entrance to commerce buildings, which among other uses was the Kings Arms Hotel and the post office. It was another fine classical building designed by W. Hindle. Removed to enable footpath widening, the columns were purchased by the council in 1879.[15]

Going through the Keresforth Hall Road entrance into the park you get to choose alternative routes. The Valley Gardens, also known as the Serpentine Walk, leads you through a former sandstone quarry past an ornamental fountain presented to Miss McCreery by the working men of Barnsley in 1877. At the end of the gardens are the ABC steps containing consecutive letters. Ascending from the quarry you instantly see the four giant relocated stone columns that, were it not for the weather, could be the imagined ruins of the Ionic Temple of Ilissus in Athens. It was fashionable at the time for gentlemen to go on a 'grand tour' and as a result the architecture of ancient Greece and Rome was often imitated. James Stuart and Nicolas Revett carried out a survey of Athens and published *Twenty-two Prints of the Antiquities of Athens* in 1751. Four volumes of prints were published in total, which provided pattern books to inspire many classical buildings.

23. Joseph Locke Monument

Joseph Locke attended Barnsley Grammar School and due to his father's close friendship with George Stephenson he became his unpaid apprentice. When Joseph Locke died in September 1860 the *Times* obituary described him as completing the triumvirate of the engineering world, along with Brunel and Robert Stephenson, who had both died in 1859. His portrait, which hangs in the Institution of Civil Engineers, was painted by the President of the Royal Academy, Sir Francis Grant in

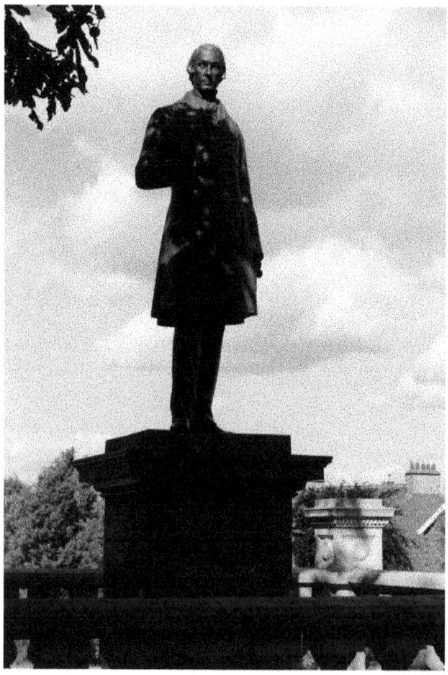

Carlo Marochetti produced some of the country's most celebrated monuments, including those of Brunel and Robert Stephenson.

1838. Also on display here is a painting from 1848 showing a group of engineers, which includes the triumvirate, sat in front of the Menia Bridge.

While not as revered in England, in France Locke was very highly regarded. He was responsible for railway lines from Paris to Rouen and Rouen to Le Harve, which required a bridge with eight arches over the River Seine. Locke's Mirville Valley Viaduct comprised fifty-two arches.

Queen Victoria attended the grand inauguration of the Caen to Cherbourg Railway. At the same lavish function Emperor Napoleon III conferred the Cross of Officer of the Legion of Honour on Locke and a replica of the statue in Locke Park was erected in 1951 at Barentin where the viaduct he built is named after him.[16]

The Joseph Locke Monument stands above the serpentine fountain on top of wide stone steps. The statue's creator was Baron Carlo Marochetti (1805–67), a celebrated Italian-born sculptor who ranked among the favourite artists of Queen Victoria and Prince Albert.

Locke's ambition was to obtain a higher place in society. He had boasted about becoming an MP when still a teenager. Locke purchased the manor house in Honition, Devon, a town that had only 300 eligible voters but returned two MPs. Locke was duly elected in 1847. Unfortunately, his independent views on a range of matters, including supporting electoral reform in Barnsley, upset the government.

Locke's statue was to be erected in the gardens of St Margaret's, Westminster, but due to his outspoken views in Parliament this was blocked. A memorial window installed in Westminster Abbey was later removed and is now stored at Cannon Hall Museum. Therefore, as Barnsley was the one place anxious to honour its famous son it has this monument by one of the most eminent sculptors in the world – he also produced the Richard the Lionheart statue in the grounds of Westminster.

24. Penistone Viaduct

The railways built by Joseph Locke impacted greatly on the British landscape. Ruskin, who wrote about his dislike of railway construction, complained about 'brutally amputated hills'.[17] Perhaps Locke's greatest engineering feat was to design the Lancaster to Carlisle Railway, which opened in 1846. This required a route over the most difficult terrain in the country, the Lakeland Fells of Cumbria. William Wordsworth objected to the damaging impact the line would have on the Lake District's natural beauty and Locke was reported to have had meetings with the poet.[18]

However, these vast engineering works are now fully integrated into the landscape. One of Locke's assistants was Alfred Jee and among his works for Locke was the Huddersfield and Sheffield line. This required three viaducts at Lockwood, Denby Dale and Penistone. The Penistone Viaduct, which traverses the Don Valley, is next to the town's station some 8 miles west of Barnsley.

The viaduct was opened in 1850 and contains twenty-eight round arches on two stage piers, with an additional arch over the Sheffield to Halifax road. With a 300-metre span it is one of the longest viaducts in the country. The arches vary in height, but the viaduct is roughly 24 metres high and around 10 metres wide to accommodate two railway lines.

The Huddersfield train was regularly held on the viaduct, which is only 30 metres from Penistone station. To save time people would get off and walk along the track, but on 9 September 1884 a passenger fell to his death. Thinking the train had arrived at the station, short-sighted Elliott Hawkyard stepped over the parapet.

After a failure to act on reports of a crack in the parapet a 30-yard section of the viaduct collapsed on the afternoon of 3 February in 1916 and an empty engine plummeted into the valley below. While the driver and fireman were able to run

The viaduct provides a dramatic backdrop for the adjacent Watermeadows Park.

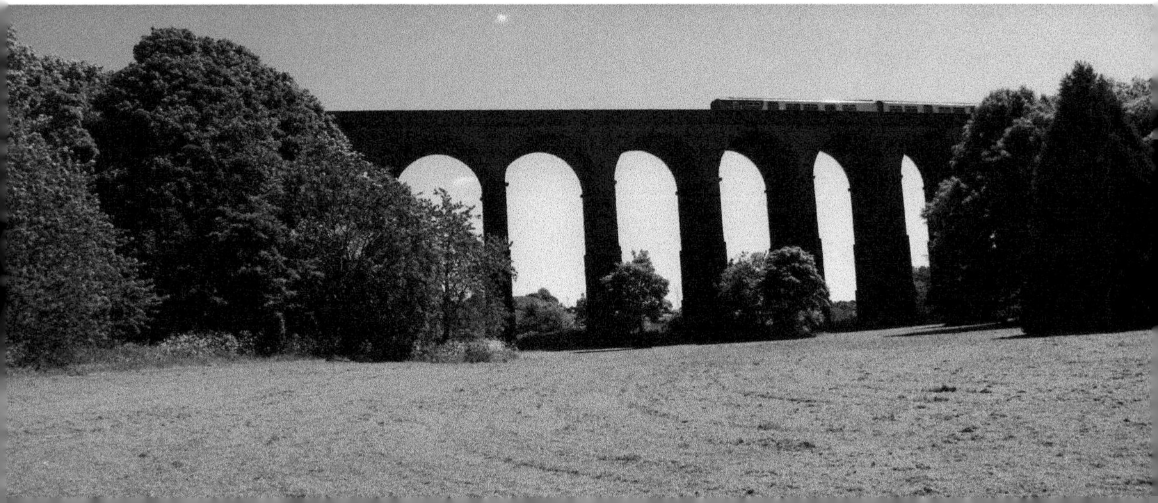

for safety just in time, had the crowded Huddersfield train passed over the viaduct there would have been considerable loss of life. The chimney of the engine was salvaged and taken to nearby Brockholes station and used as a flowerpot.[19]

25. Locke Tower

Built in 1875–77 on the highest point in Barnsley, the observation tower was designed by Richard Phene Spiers for Sarah McCreery. This tower in Locke Park is a memorial to Phoebe Locke. Spiers was to become master of the Royal Academy Architecture Schools and wrote extensively about architectural styles.

The Locke Tower is elaborately decorated and the tower base, comprising fourteen Ionic stone columns, supports the first-floor balcony. Above the balcony there are eight more inset columns below an overhanging entablature that supports a decorative frieze with lions' heads. At the top, the wooden lantern has a copper-clad roof.

Key elements of Locke Tower have significant similarities with the Tempietto, built in 1502 on Janiculum Hill at the site of St Peter's crucifixion in Rome. The base of Donato Bramante's diminutive but perfectly formed dome is replicated in the monument.

The tower originally had a weathervane at the apex of the lantern with Sarah McCreery's monogram. Unfortunately, the weathervane blew off in a storm,

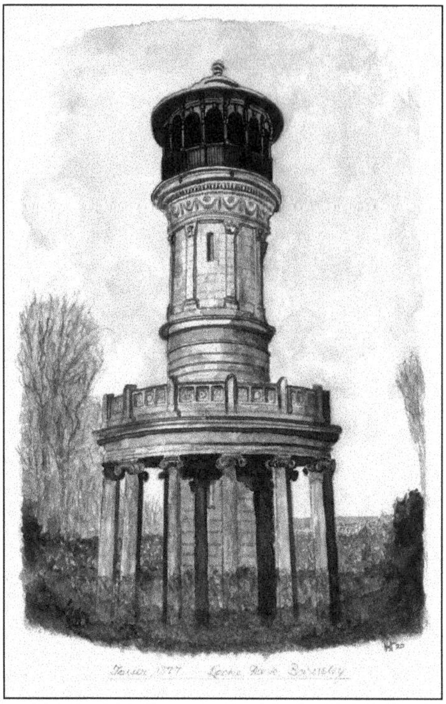

This classic folly was built to provide panoramic views of the park.

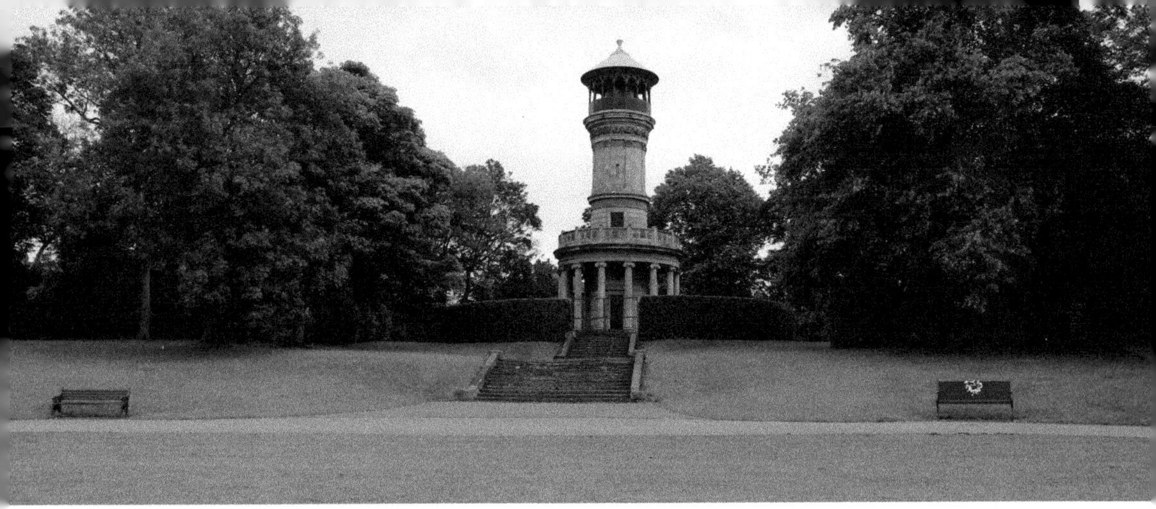

Before lockdown in 2020 the tower was open to the public one day each month.

though luckily it was reclaimed and safely stored. It is hoped to reinstate the repaired weathervane as part of future renovations.

There is a circular hedge around the base of the tower with cast-iron gates. Two flights of stone steps set in grass embankments lead down to a terrace and seating area. The tower, which is the main feature of Locke Park, is a classic folly. A folly, also called an eyecatcher, is erected purely to enhance a natural landscape. There are many different types of folly, but the most common form is a tower to facilitate views of the landscape. Locke tower, which is around 21 metres tall, has a circular central staircase to a first-floor balcony below a lantern.

In industrial towns like Barnsley, workers who spent most of their week underground or in noisy factories and mills wanted on their one day off to get dressed up and go out into the countryside. At the same time Victorian reformers believed that the working classes needed formal, more ordered leisure activity, and public parks were seen as an integral part of this approach. Pavilions, bowling greens, paddling pools, glass houses and bandstands were provided to encourage the labouring class into parks and out of gin palaces and pubs.

26. The Bandstand

The cast-iron bandstand is set on a low brick base with stone coping. There are eight ornamental columns supporting an arcaded freeze and a domed roof with a lead-covered central cap.

Most bandstands found in parks and open spaces were manufactured near Glasgow, where the iron ore was perfect for cast iron. Therefore, it is no surprise that the Locke Park bandstand comes from the Lion Foundry Co. Ltd, Kirkintilloch.

Bandstands like the one at Locke Park quickly became hugely popular attractions. Paintings by L. S. Lowry of the bandstand in his local park in Salford show large crowds comprising hundreds of people. At the official opening on

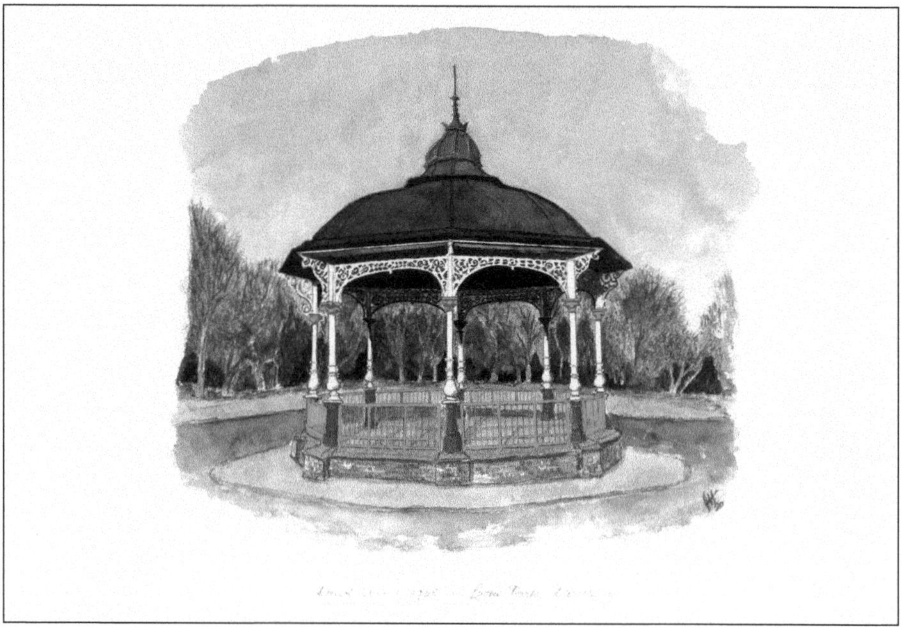

The bandstand is the centrepiece of an open-air venue.

11 June 1908 the Barnsley Volunteers Band played to 25,000 people.[20] In their heyday there were over 1,500 bandstands in Britain – in public parks, on piers and seaside promenades.

There is a strong tradition of brass bands in the Barnsley area and bands were originally either works bands or sponsored by various industrial concerns. This

The Locke Park bandstand was installed in 1908 at a cost of £326.

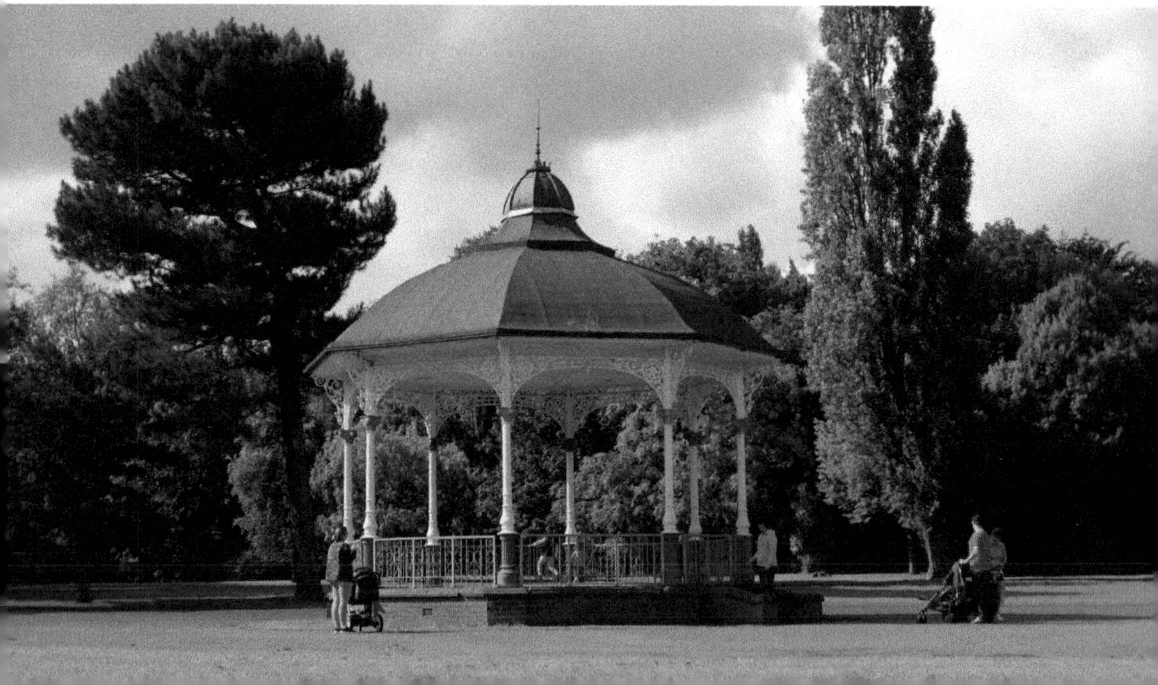

was particularly evident in coal mining areas, and a year prior to the bandstand being installed the Barnsley Borough Town Band tasted success at the prestigious National Brass Band festival at Crystal Palace. The most famous band in the Barnsley area is the Grimethope Colliery Band. They have played at the Albert Hall Proms and performed with international singing stars, but are most well known for their role in the film *Brassed Off*.

Bands from areas close to Locke Park would have included the Gawber Village Band, which was formed in 1868, and the Old Silkstone Band, established in 1861. There were also a number of brass bands based in Dodworth, including a Rifle Corps Band formed in 1863.[21]

Locke Park was also the venue for the National Union of Mineworkers (Yorkshire Area) Annual Demonstration and Gala. This comprised a long procession that included no less than forty-six brass bands headed by pipes and drums. The procession started marching from the Miners Hall, Keir Street and Churchfields. In June 1947, Prime Minister Clement Atlee and Minister of Power Emmanuel 'Manny' Shinwell were in Barnsley as speakers and guests at the Yorkshire Miners' Gala. Before the march to Locke Park they were given a civic reception at the Town Hall. The 1965 Gala included speeches from Labour cabinet minister George Brown, a brass band concert and finished off with the crowning of the Coal Queen.

27. National Union of Mineworkers Offices

The National Union of Mineworkers Offices occupy a prestigious corner site at the heart of a conservation area. This impressive building was built in 1874 for the South Yorkshire and Derbyshire Miners' Association and was designed by Wade and Turner in a French Gothic style with a prominent corner apse. This features two round towers, the larger having a decorated conical roof crowned with an intricate finial.

While they were the first trade union offices to be built in the country, they were not then the national headquarters. Other coalfield areas had their own headquarters. The South Yorkshire Miners' Association was formed at a meeting in the Old White Bear Inn, Shambles Street, on 5 April 1858. The NUM offices were originally two houses, one for the president and the other for the branch secretary, with the offices in the central section. The principal entrance has a grand triumphal arch; the second has a simple square stone porch.

Presidents who lived at the NUM offices include workhouse boy Herbert Smith, who held office from 1906 until his death at his desk in the NUM offices in 1938. Famously being a man of few words, during the 1926 General Strike he said, 'Now't doin' when Prime Minister Stanley Baldwin proposed to increase miners' hours and cut their pay.

Vesting Day on 1 January 1947 was when the new National Coal Board took control of the country's 1,647 mines. The miners' working week was cut to five

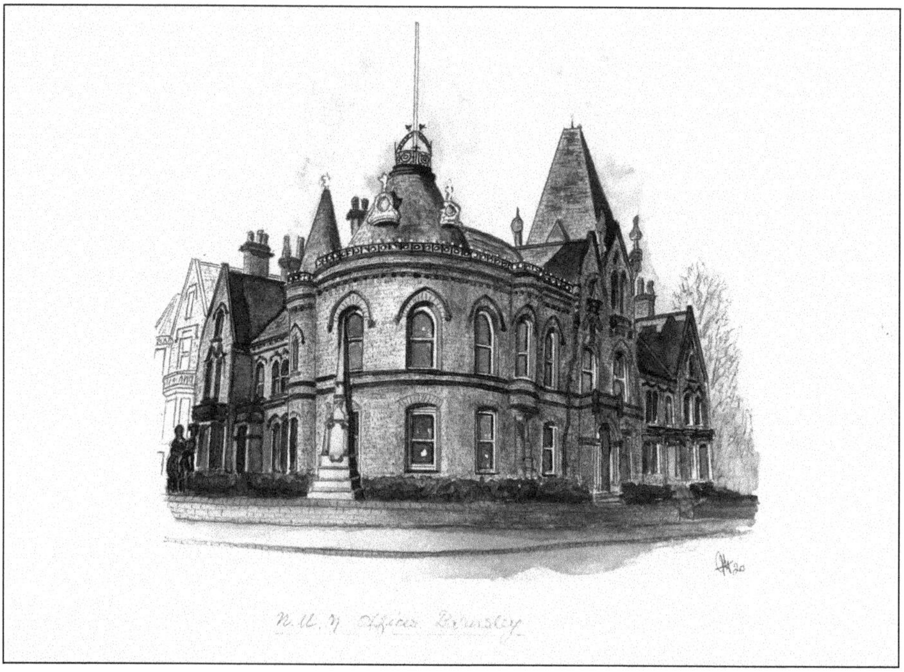

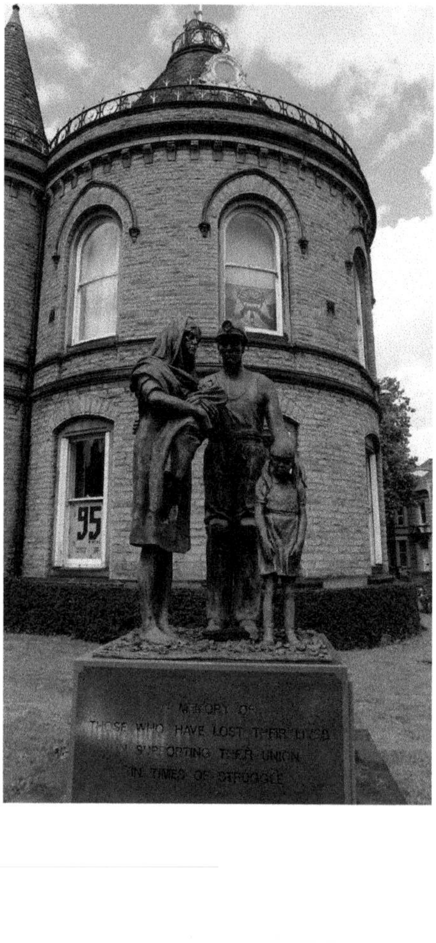

Above: The offices are a 'gateway building' at the northern entrance to the town centre.

Left: A bronze Graham Ibbotson sculpture is dedicated to those who died supporting the Miners Union.

days and working conditions were improved. However, accidents still occurred, and at the Yorkshire Miners' Gala in front of the Town Hall in June 1975 a black ribbon was draped on the Houghton Main banner due to an accident where five miners were killed shortly before the gala.

Coal and its by-products were key to Barnsley's prosperity. In October 1992, a national 'Pit Closure Programme' was announced, in which thirty-one pits were to be closed. A 'Fight for Coal' rally packed Barnsley town Centre on 7 November and schoolchildren from Willowgarth School, Grimethorpe, went to Downing Street to hand in protest letters. Nevertheless, Grimethorpe Colliery closed in May 1993 and the old colliery complex was demolished in 1994. While coal is no longer mined in the Barnsley area, legacy issues can adversely impact the viability of potential development sites.

28. The Miners Hall

This is one of Barnsley's hidden gems. Its stunning interior would normally be seen in a grand public building such as a town hall. The NUM offices and Miners Hall are two separate buildings connected via an internal bridge link. The public entrance to the Miners Hall is on Victoria Road. This is a truly superb space with a decorative suspended ceiling and has what appears to be natural light coming in through skylights, but it is actually from electric lights in the roof above.

The year the Miners Hall was completed (1912) saw both the sinking of the *Titanic* and Barnsley's only FA cup triumph. In the same year George V visited Barnsley, having stayed as the guest of local mine owner the Earl of Fitzwilliam at Wentworth Woodhouse.

The hall is home to the NUM archive and is a place where many union banners are on display, including some over 100 years old. The oldest is for the Lofthouse

The decorative suspended ceiling contains detailing akin to theatres of the same period.

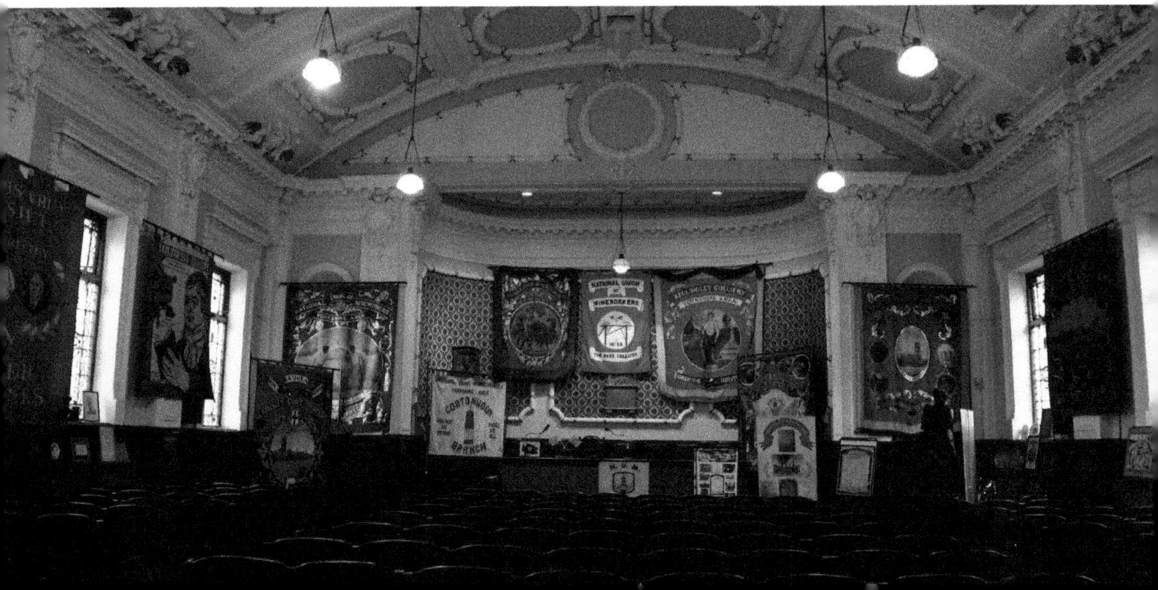

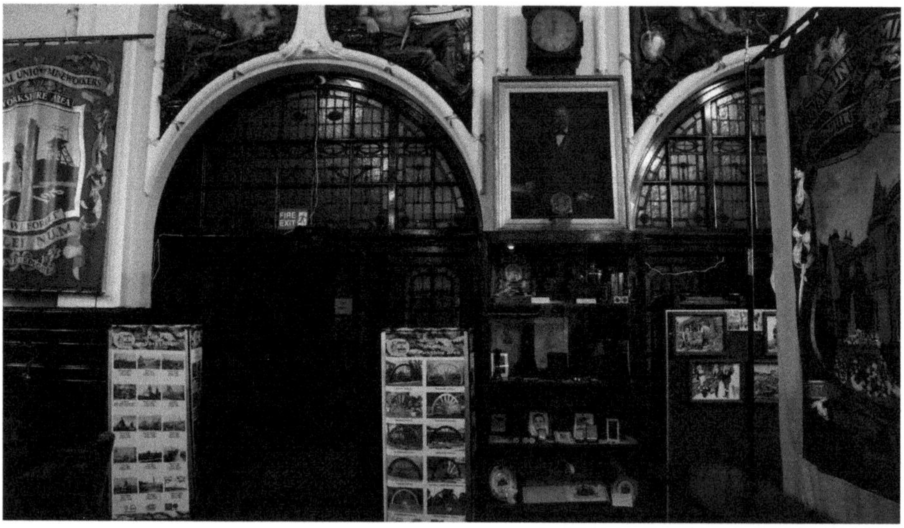

There are friezes depicting mine workers with six fingers on each hand.

Colliery from 1890, albeit repainted in 1896. Some of the banners have been repainted due to pits having been closed; another pit took the banner rather than pay to have a new one made. The Wharncliffe Silkstone banner cost £125 – a considerable sum at the time. A *Barnsley Chronicle* article from August 1987 talks about fundraising to enable restoration of the Houghton Main NUM banner with a picture of Clement Atlee and another president from the 1960s, Sam Bullough.

Next to the hall's entrance is a meeting room with paintings of former presidents and other artefacts on display. Black-and-white photos of some past presidents also adorn the entrance hallway and their names also appear on a board.

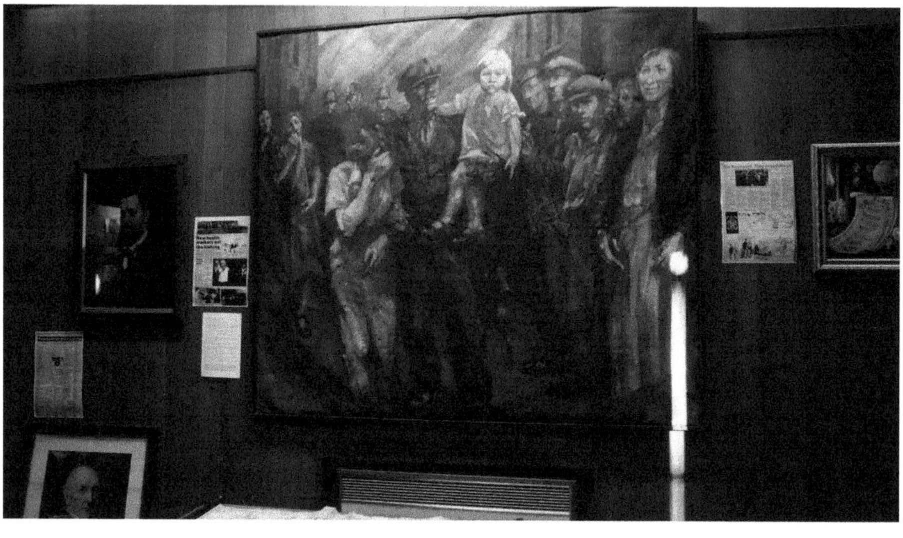

There is a meeting room with many artifacts on display.

29. Kendray Monument

The Kendray memorial was paid for by Samuel Joseph Cooper and erected in 1913 – the same year he died. It was designed by Wade and Turner and the stonemason was Peter Dalby. The bronze sculpture shows the winged goddess Athena (or Athene) supporting a fallen soldier holding a broken sword. An owl stands on the base of the sculpture, which is a copy of *Gloria Victis* (glory to the vanquished) by French artist Marius Jean Antonin Mercie.

During the nineteenth century the coal mining industry demonstrated how unrestricted capitalism was often synonymous with tragic loss of life. The history of coal mining is blighted by accidents, sometimes on a massive scale. The former Barnsley Beckett Hospital was extended specifically to deal with the increase in coal mining injuries. However, it was not until the 1919 Coal Mining Act that rescue teams became a requirement for all collieries.

The worst mining disaster in England took place at Oaks Colliery, Hoyle Mill, in 1866. On 12 December an explosion killed 334 men and boys. On 13 December a second, larger explosion killed the rescuers. One of the twenty-seven rescuers killed was Parkin Jeffcock, and St Saviour's Church in High Green Sheffield was built in 1872 as a memorial to him.

The next day Samuel Brown, one of the rescuers, was famously rescued by J. E. Mammatt and T. E. Embleton. However, on the same day it was decided no one else would be left alive and the shafts were filled up and pumps were

The memorial is located on the brow of a hill opposite the impressive Kendray Hospital.

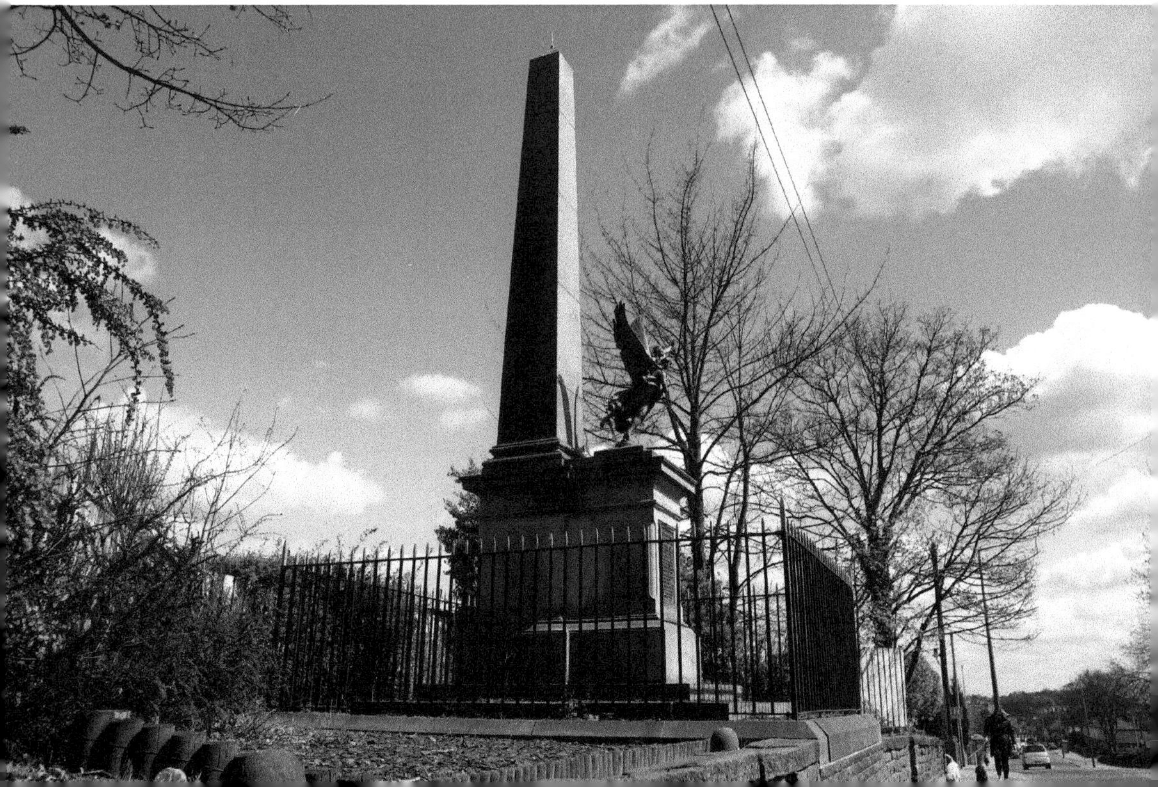

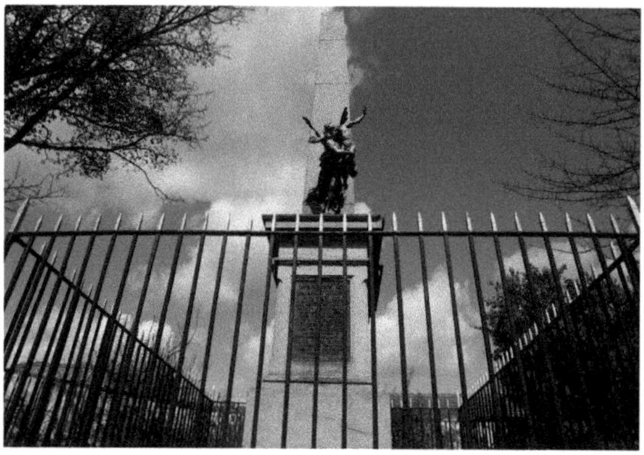

The Oaks Monument statue was restored by Sheffield sculptor Chris Bolton in 1992.

started to ensure the mine was not flooded. There are still 169 unrecovered bodies under the ground where the pit was located. Explosions kept occurring for weeks afterwards, and there was a massive impact on the local community. At Hoyle Mill cottages only one of the families did not lose someone.

The coroner's inquest started at the Old White Bear in Hoyle Mill and the *Manchester Times* reported that the Archbishop of York and Earl Fitzwilliam visited the pit and surrounding homes where nearly all were in mourning. This inquest was adjourned and a second was held at the courthouse on Regent Street. The verdict was that firedamp gas had caused the explosion, but there would be no prosecutions or changes in legislation to prevent another disaster. It was not until 1872 that a new Coal Mining Regulations Act was passed.[22]

3c. Oaks Colliery Disaster Memorial

The first memorial to the disaster was erected in 1879 at Christ Church, Ardsley. There is also a mining-related stained-glass window installed inside the church. However, as there was no national memorial to the miners killed at Oaks a group of former miners, supported by the National Union of Mineworkers, raised money for a statue.

A poem was written by Barnsley poet Ian McMillan to mark the anniversary and a special service took place at St Mary's Church. The film *Black Snow* won the Best Research Film of the Year award at the 2018 BAFTAs. In the film, Graham Ibbotson says the sculpture is the endgame of his career.

A banner for the Oaks Colliery (1847–66) is on display at the Miners Hall, as is the initial scaled model of the Oaks Disaster Monument. The work shows a mother with a child in her arms, her hair extending in the form of coal down her back. There is a large steel halo, which alludes to the pit winding gear, but according to the sculptor this represents the circle of life. Below the female figure, her husband is seen 'digging his own grave'. A separate plinth outlines the history of the disaster.

Artworks shed light on past events, which can in some cases be divisive, as seen with the 1895 statue of slave trader Edward Coulson being thrown into

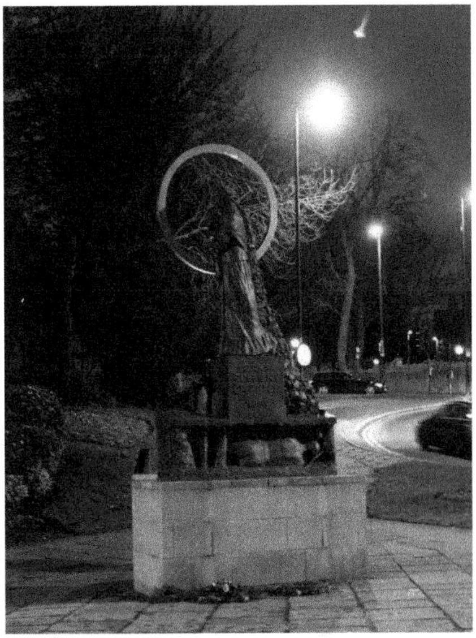

Sculptor Graham Ibbotson's relative George Ibbotson was killed in the first blast.

Bristol's floating harbour at Pero's Bridge (named after an enslaved African) on 7 June 2020. Often the public realm can be the best means of education, and this monument is a fine example of how such a catastrophic event can be encapsulated by a skilled artist.

31. Barnsley Main

Being located in an isolated, windswept spot Barnsley Main has an evocative, almost eerie, presence. This is the last significant surviving structure with some historical connection to the Oaks Colliery Disaster. The Oaks Colliery pithead was actually to the south-east, now within an industrial estate. However, by 1931 Barnsley Main Colliery had expanded, taking over Oaks Colliery.

As would be expected from a working mine, the disused colliery winding engine house and pithead structures are made up of parts dating from various periods. Before nationalisation the Barnsley Main Colliery No. 2 Shaft was originally part of Rylands Main Colliery. Dan Rylands bought the site in 1890, and the earliest definitive record of any associated buildings are shown on the Ordnance Survey map published in 1906.

The national importance of coal mining came into sharp focus during the Second World War and reconstruction of aging pits was a priority. The mine was modernised and reconstructed in 1956 by the National Coal Board, involving the construction of the upper floor of the engine house and the upper part of the shaft-head building. There is a date stone on the engine house to mark this modernisation. The colliery closed and reopened many times, but it finally ceased production permanently in 1991.

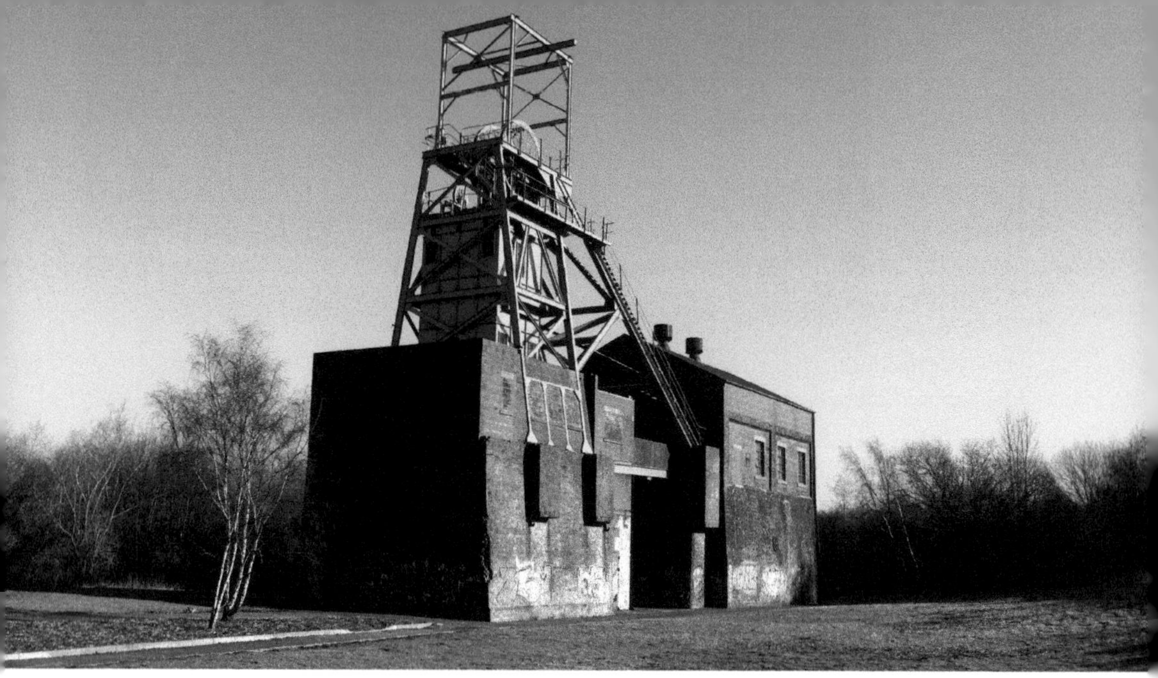

It is claimed that Barnsley Main is haunted by victims of the Oaks disaster.

It is a poignant reminder of the coal industry in Barnsley – the most significant industrial heritage of the town. It is particularly important considering that most other complete pithead structures have been removed from across the South Yorkshire Coalfield.

The winding gear was made by Needham Brothers and Browns Ltd on Pontefract Road. In 1994, after 118 years, the business was acquired by Barnsley-based Qualter, Hall & Company Ltd. Parts of the pithead winding gear have been preserved to mark where mines used to exist at various locations around Barnsley. Television news recently reported anger in Grimethorpe when a preserved pit wheel was moved from its prominent main road location to accommodate a housing development.

There are railway tracks retained next to the building and nearby is one of the few remaining parts of the Barnsley Canal, showing how important early canal and railway development was to the growth of the coal mining industry.

32. The Former York Street Baths

At the opening of the town's public baths on 15 June 1874, Mayor C. Newman said that while growing up he bathed in the Old Dyke or the Barnsley Canal.[23] With a closely packed population, overcrowded workers' homes in central Barnsley lacked basic facilities. *The Lancet* published a report dated 25 January 1908 entitled 'Barnsley Disaster: Dissemination of Enteric Fever due to a "Typhoid Carrier"'.

This attractive Italian Gothic building designed by Wade and Turner has an ashlar stone front, dressed stone on the sides and rear and a Welsh slate roof. Male and female slipper baths were provided – towels were draped across the bathers to protect their modesty, making them look like slippers.

The white-tiled swimming pool with a diamond pattern in black tiles was bounded by thirty-two dressing cubicles. A viewing gallery with ornamental railings was supported by cast-iron pillars.[24] By 1914 the York Street baths were overcrowded so a second bath house with a bigger pool was erected. This had a grand, colonnaded entrance onto Race Street and seating for between 600 and 700 people. There were twenty-four slipper baths and a laundry.

Watching northern-based, kitchen sink drama films from the early 1960s such as *This Sporting Life,* the industrial towns featured had tall chimneys and dance halls and the 'Townend Baths' are a reminder of the social history of the town.

With so many linen mills concentrated in this part of Barnsley, high chimneys were a major feature in the townscape. The 1893 map shows Taylor's Mill on Peel Street, Hope Works on Sackville Street, Boar Spring Mill on Pitt Street and Oak Mill on Plumber Street. None of these buildings remain, so the chimney at the former baths, with its square at base, octagonal top with bands, deep moulded cornice and ashlar cap is a reminder of this industrial heritage.

By installing a temporary maple floor over the pool, regular dances and public meetings were held. It was reported that the maple floor had an extra spring because it was not solid underneath. The Ambassadors, with *Emmerdale* actor Stan Richards on piano, were a regular dance band.[25]

The Race Street Baths were demolished in 1989 and the York Street baths converted to residential use.

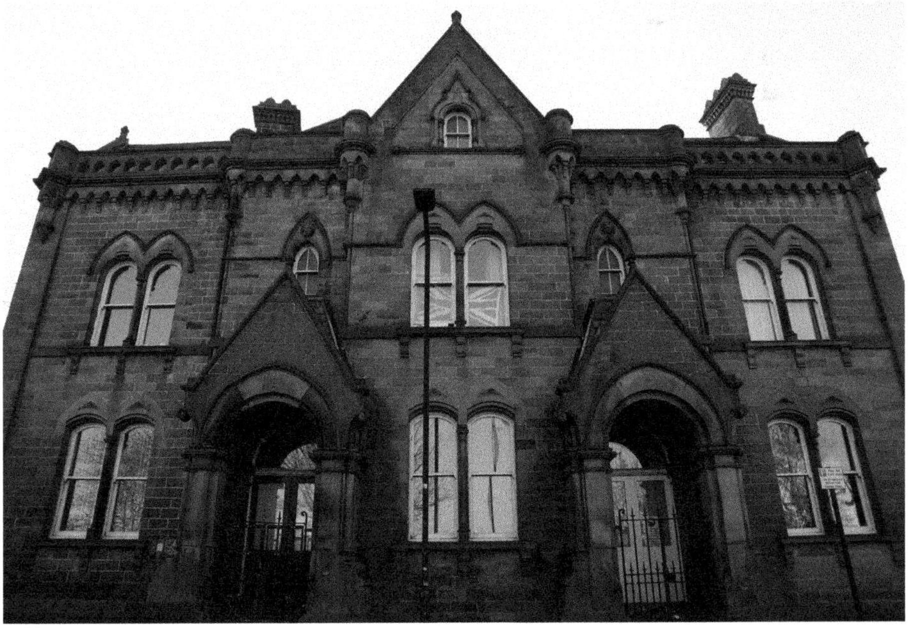

Male and female entrances with gabled porches – it was only in 1927 that mixed bathing was allowed.

33. The Civic Theatre

This is one of the most decorative buildings in Barnsley. It is a baroque-style building designed by Hill & Swan of Leeds, and the elaborate eaves detailing is the standout feature. The figurehead of benefactor Charles Harvey of Park House, Kendray, hovers over the Eldon Street entrance in an enlarged keystone.

When it opened in February 1878 this impressive building was called the Barnsley Mechanics' Institute and Public Hall. The first Barnsley Mechanics' Institute opened in 1883 and moved to various locations. The new building was an upgrade that included a lecture hall, reading room, library, museum and classrooms. To provide additional income there were also shops and offices. Charles Harvey handed the building to the town and it was renamed the Harvey Institute in 1890.

In 1962, the building became a traditional proscenium arch theatre seating 800 people. It hosted some big name shows and many local Operatic Society performances. In the 1970s pop groups including the Real Thing, Mud and Bay City Rollers played there. Local comedian Charlie Williams performed here regularly, but the theatre closed in 1998.

In 2008, a plaque was installed near the Eldon Street entrance showing the names of the children who died in a tragic accident that occurred at the Public Hall on Saturday 11 January 1908. Sixteen died and forty were injured when more children than anticipated turned up to watch a penny showing of a film. To deal with a crush on the balcony the attendant directed children down a narrow staircase to the main hall. However, the pressure of children pushing from the rear caused those at the front to trip and they were trampled.

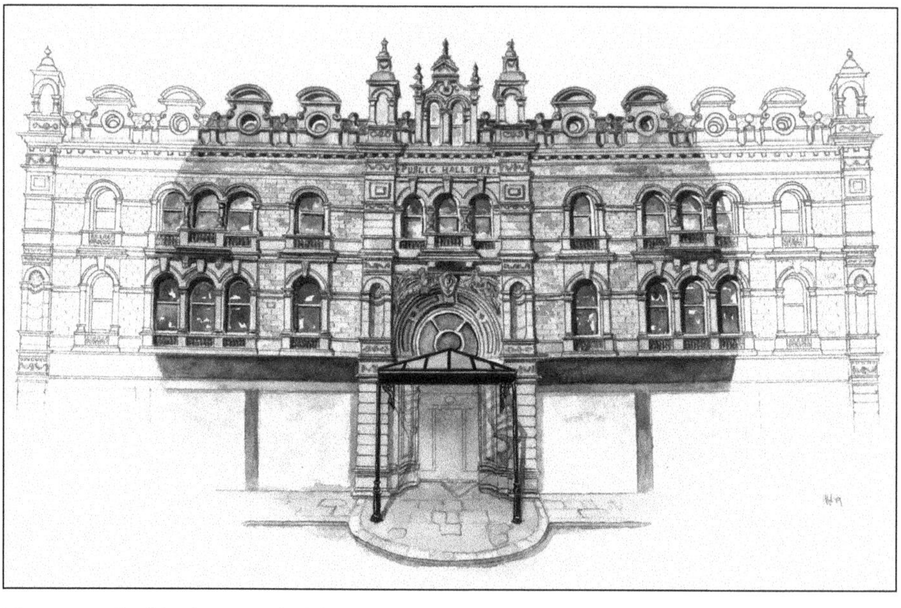

The ornate highly decorated Eldon Street frontage is one of the finest in Barnsley.

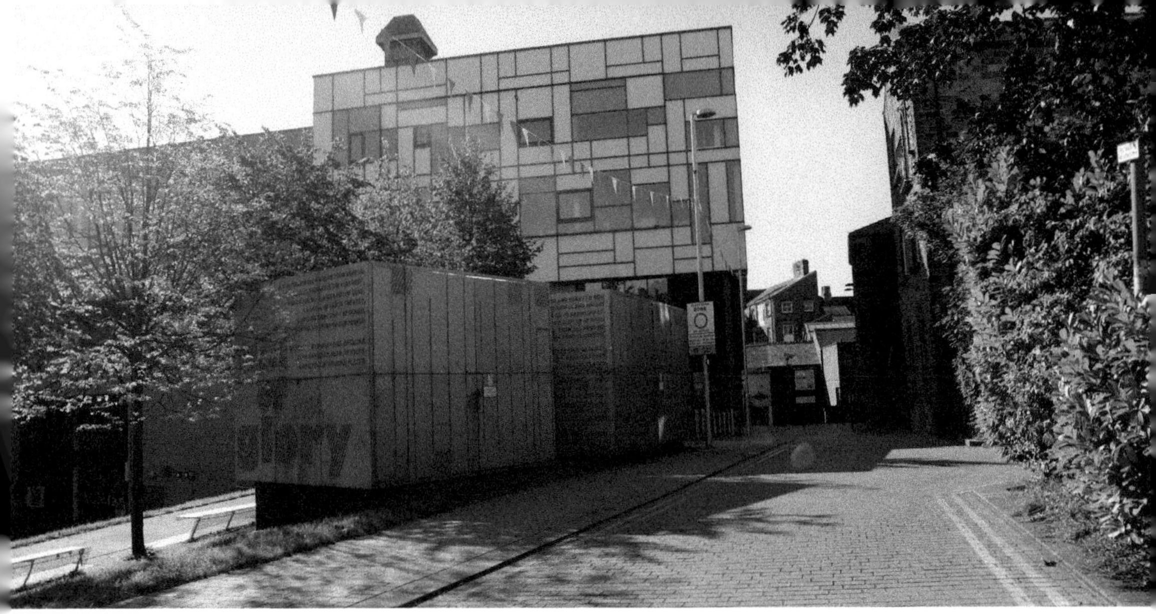

The new performance area is accessed from Hanson Street.

After major refurbishment a reduced-size 384-seat performance space known as the Assembly Room was opened in March 2009. Parts of the decorative ceiling and walls of the theatre were retained in the new ground-level performance space with retractable tiered seating. Access is from George Yard and Hanson Street via an attractive glazed panel extension abutting Mandela Gardens. 'Full of Glory' is a poem that features on a substation covered with silver screens near the entrance to the refurbished building, which also includes a contemporary gallery, café and function rooms.

It is now hoped that £7 million will be spent on the Civic in part to reinstate a box office on the Eldon Street entrance.

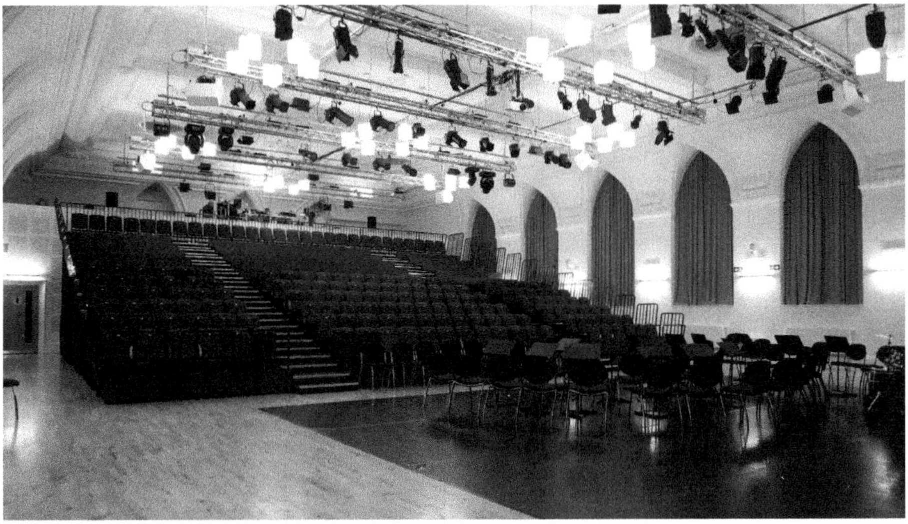

The original carved and moulded plasterwork is retained in the new auditorium.

34. Oakwell Stadium

At the foot of Whin Bank, the Oakwell was a spring located at Beevor Hole. In 1813, Willian Jackson purchased Beevor Hole with James Lister and used the spring water for linen manufacture.

Barnsley Football Club was founded in 1887 by the clergyman Tiverton Preedy, who named the team Barnsley St Peter's after a nearby church. Oakwell became their home ground in 1888. In 1897, the club changed its name to Barnsley FC, but locally they are known as 'the Tykes'. They were early joiners of the Football League in 1898 and have played mostly in the lower leagues. However, some footballing greats have played at Barnsley. Barnsley-born goal machine Tommy Taylor was killed at the age of just twenty-six in the Munich air disaster. His scoring statistics for England were sixteen goals in just nineteen appearances.

Barnsley FC's headquarters were located in the Clarence Hotel on Sheffield Road, and it is here in 1912 that they celebrated the club's only FA Cup victory over West Bromwich Albion. The first game at Crystal Palace was a 0-0 draw and the replay took place at Bramall Lane, Sheffield, in front of 33,000 fans. Wembley would not open until 1923.

The record attendance was 42,056 for a game against Stoke City in 1935. In the previous season they put nine goals past Accrington Stanley without reply and they would go on to be crowned champions of Division Three North. They would do this again in 1938/39 and 1954/55.[26]

In a clip on YouTube from the 1970s Michael Parkinson and Brian Glover are talking about being spectators. It shows how the ground looked at a time when it had a capacity of 38,500. This was before all seater stadiums and when only 15,000 seats were under cover and the Spion Kop was a bank made of waste from a nearby coking plant.

The 1920/21 season ended with Barnsley in the Championship play-offs.

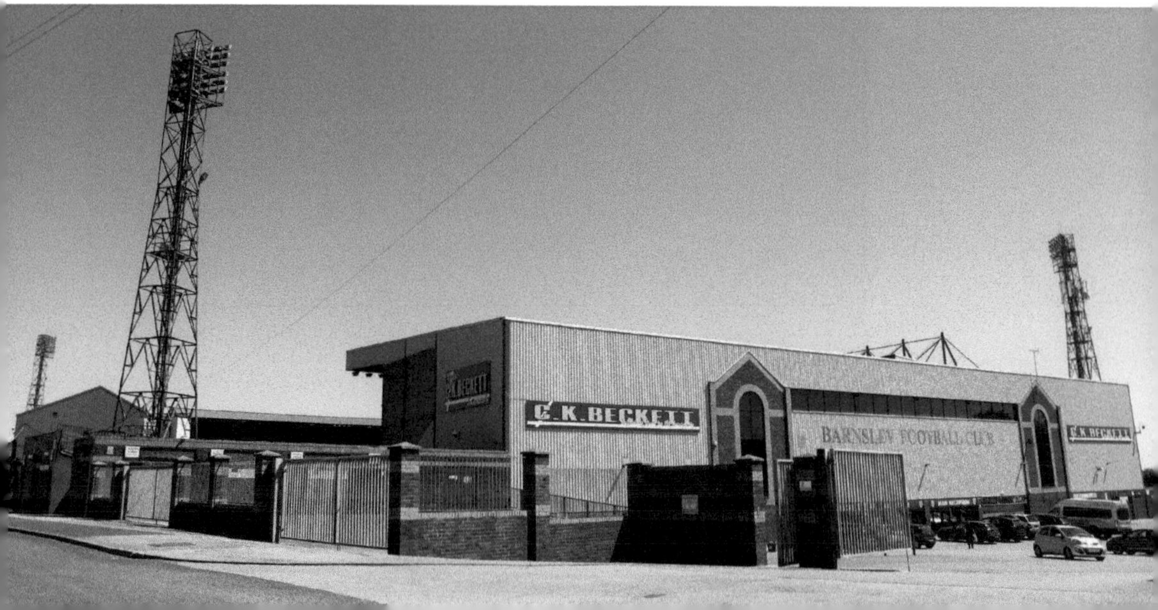

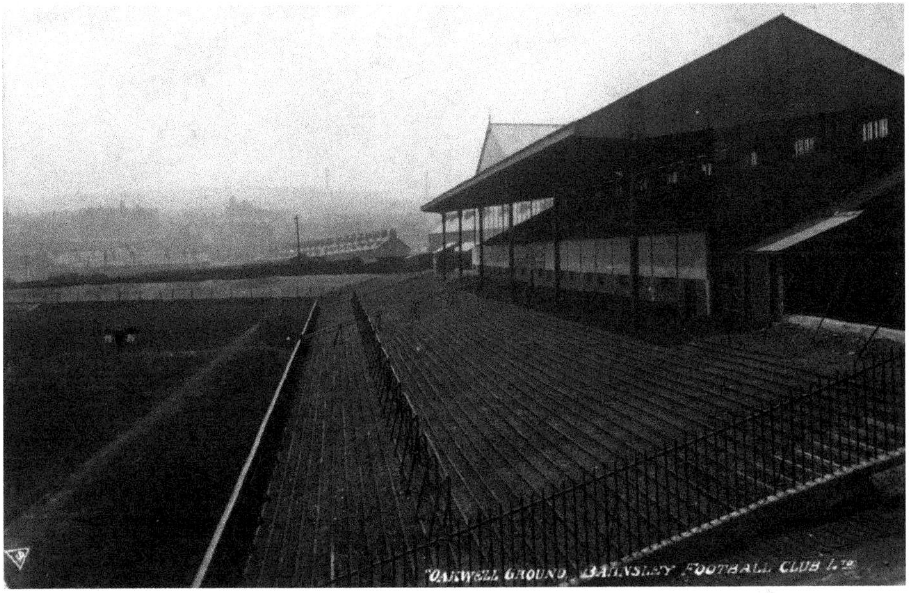

Oakwell in 1960 when most spectators were outside in all weathers.

The fans had to wait until 1997 for their next major achievement, when the Tykes clinched promotion to the Premier League. While Barnsley lasted just one glorious season in the Premier League, it was claimed they played like Brazil.

Oakwell, which now has a seating capacity of 23,287, was the first stadium in English football to have a designated stand for disabled supporters. Notwithstanding the modernisation it is one of the few remaining old-style grounds comprising four separate stands with floodlights on towers in the corners.

35. The Church of St Peter the Apostle and John the Baptist

Looking up from Oakwell Stadium, this imposing red-brick building is a highly prominent feature on the hillside along with the nearby Oakwell View Primary School, built in 1905. This is highly appropriate given that Barnsley FC began life as Barnsley St Peter's.

The parish church of St Peter the Apostle and John the Baptist is of the Anglo-Catholic tradition. It is stated that people have worshipped on this site since 1872 and that the church was built using penny contributions from the local mining families. The church was built between 1893 and 1911 indicating a pre-existing church building was the base for Barnsley FC. The church is set within high-density terraced houses and forms an integral part of the community it serves.

This imposing red-brick church is among the finest buildings in South Yorkshire and was recognised as such by Nikolaus Pevsner. St Peter's was designed by Temple Lushington Moore, an Irish-born architect who specialised in Gothic

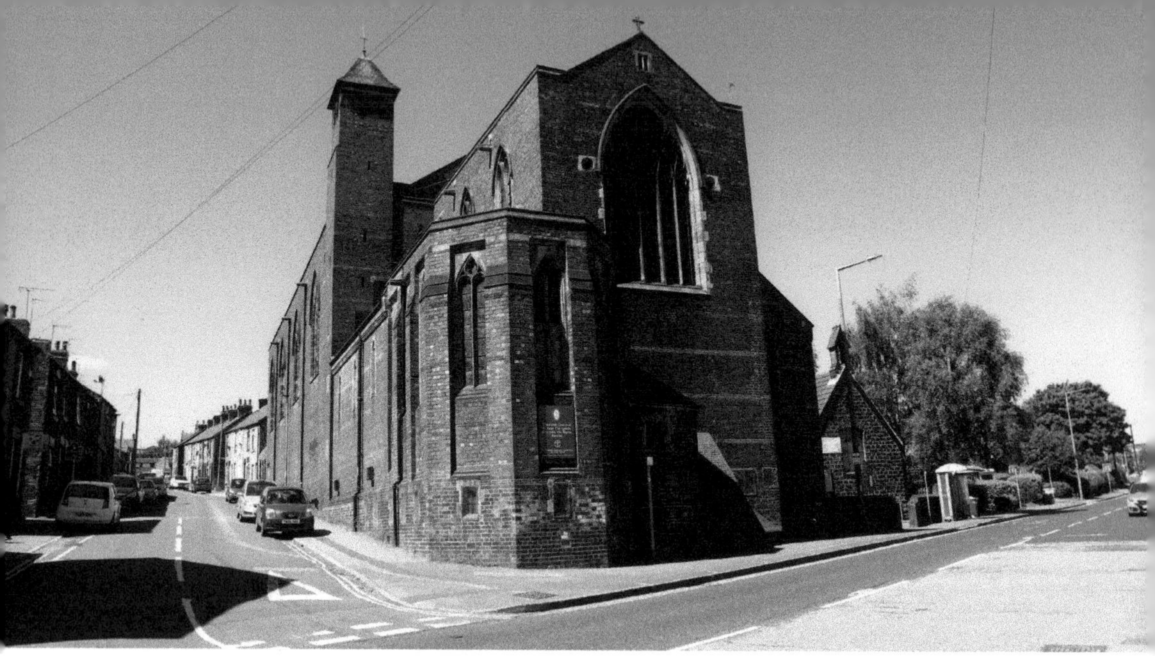

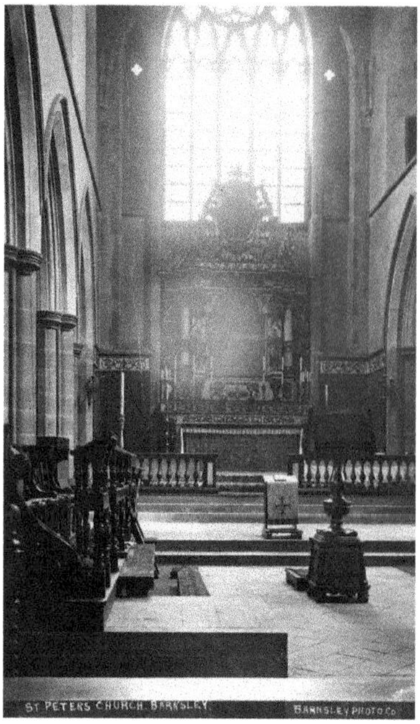

Above: The scale of the church can be judged against the adjacent St Peter's Church Hall.

Left: The high altar is illuminated by the superb stained-glass window.

Revival churches. In England there was a thirst for medieval romance in literature and after 1820 there was a surge in Gothic houses and churches. Temple Moore was influenced by a leading exponent of the Gothic Revival, Sir George Gilbert Scott, who designed the Albert Memorial and the St Pancras Midland Hotel. Temple Moore then taught Giles Gilbert Scott, who went on to design Liverpool Cathedral and the classic red telephone box.

Inside the church is an intricate canopy of stone ribbed vaults suspended far overhead with Lux Nova, or new light, streaming through stained-glass windows.

The perpendicular emphasis encloses the maximum amount of space, and pointed arches allow in the optimal amount of light. Despite France having been the birthplace of Gothic architecture, when Abbot Suger rebuilt sections of the Basilica of Saint-Denis in the twelfth century, it is often called the 'German style'. Most of the forty churches Temple Moore designed were heavily influenced by the medieval brick churches of Germany, such as the Church of the Holy Spirit in Heidelberg.

36. Arcadia House and the Co-operative Buildings

George Adcroft was a member of the Rochdale Pioneers Society, established in 1844. When he moved to work at Oaks Colliery the Barnsley British Co-operative Society was formed after 'nine men of vision' met at Tinker's Temperance Hotel, May Day Green, in August 1861. In 1865, a dwelling house, shop and grounds were purchased on Wellington Street for the society.

There were three grand Co-operative buildings on this corner. The Arcadian Hall and Wellington House remain, but the third Co-operative building burned down in August 2016, causing the adjacent ring road to close. The site is presently a temporary car park and represents a boarded-up blemish that surely will not be allowed to detract for many more years.

Of the two remaining Co-operative buildings the Arcadian Hall is indisputably the more elaborate. On the rounded corner section there are raised art nouveau letters reading 'Barnsley British Co-operative Society Ltd'. Above this a carved lion is sat imperiously looking out over his domain.

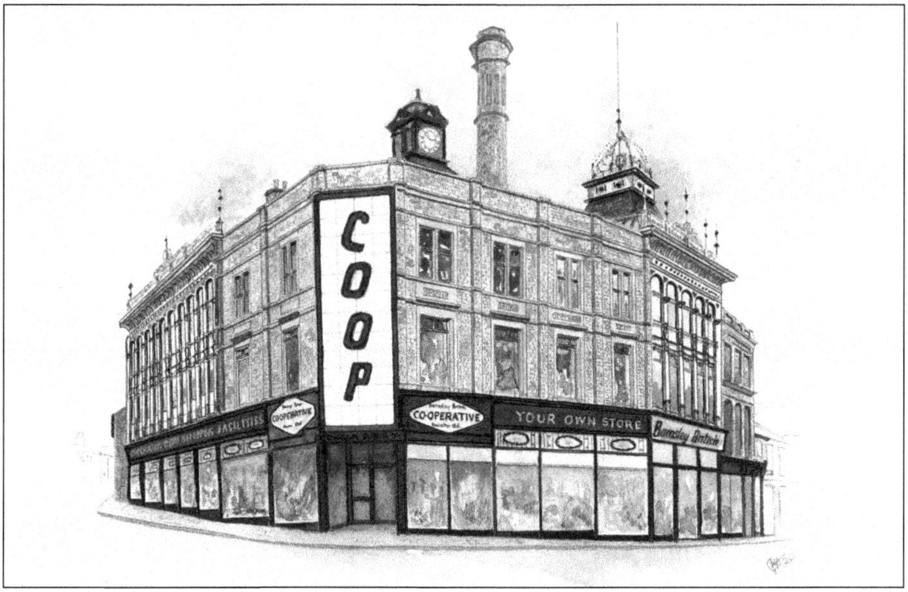

The lost 1886 Cooperative building was destroyed by a fire.

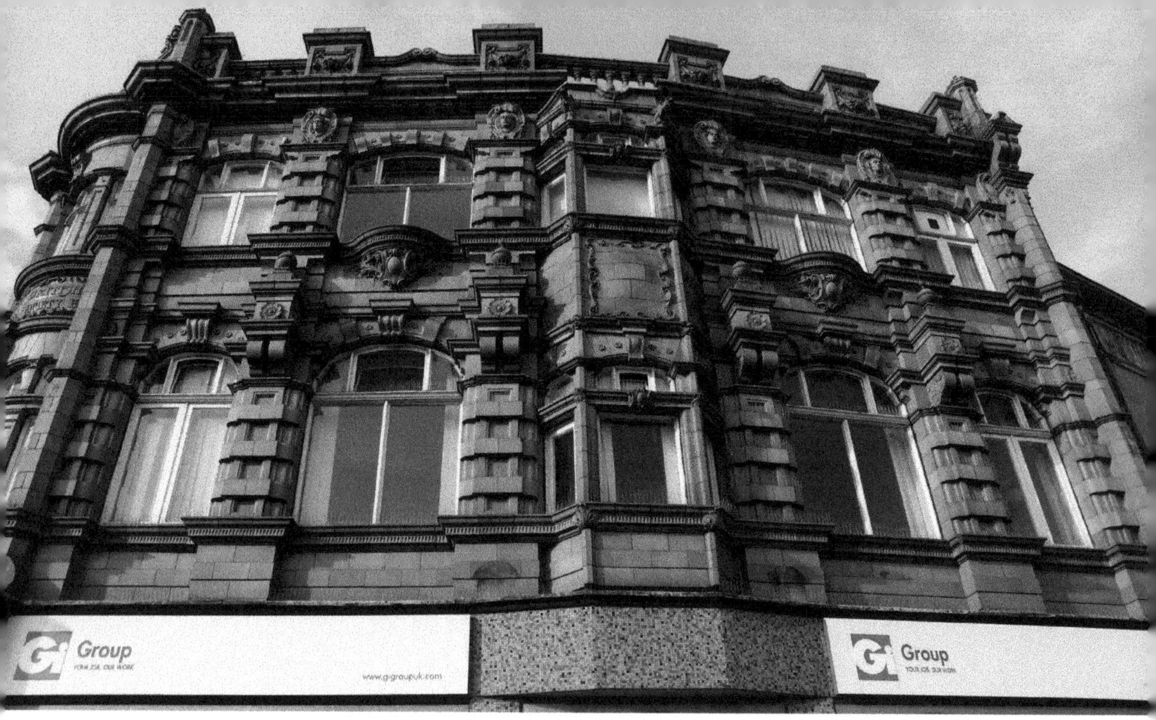

The baroque style of architecture is highly decorative and theatrical.

This excellent and decorative example of a baroque-style building dates from the end of the nineteenth century. It replaced an original building of 1865, and the premises were purchased in the 1890s by the Co-operative who used it as their central grocery department. There were traditional timber shopfronts between tiled columns. Painted signage said 'Groceries' on one side and 'Provisions' on the other. While these ground-floor frontages have been crudely modernised, the Arcadian Hall is still one of the most dramatic and exuberant buildings in Barnsley.

The detailing on the auburn façade includes a deep, moulded and modillioned (small supporting bracket) eaves cornice, which supports a parapet that is alternately panelled and balustraded. Below are cartouches (ornamental panel in the form of a scroll), voussoirs in the arched window heads, carved figureheads and a pair of projecting gargoyles. There are sophisticated horizontal and rounded elements, including bands on the columns that alternate between deep red and green.

Before being used for council offices both Wellington House and the Arcadian Hall were venues for events, concerts and dances. Wellington House was the larger venue, so the Arcadian being the smaller, more intimate venue was often used for wedding receptions and classical music recitals.

37. Theatre Royal

In its heyday the Theatre Royal provided a grand setting for audiences to see an unknown comic actor called Charlie Chaplin. The famous sand dance of Wilson Keppel and Eddy and *Coronation Street*'s Betty Driver were among the many other variety acts. An eight-year-old Julie Andrews appeared in 1943.

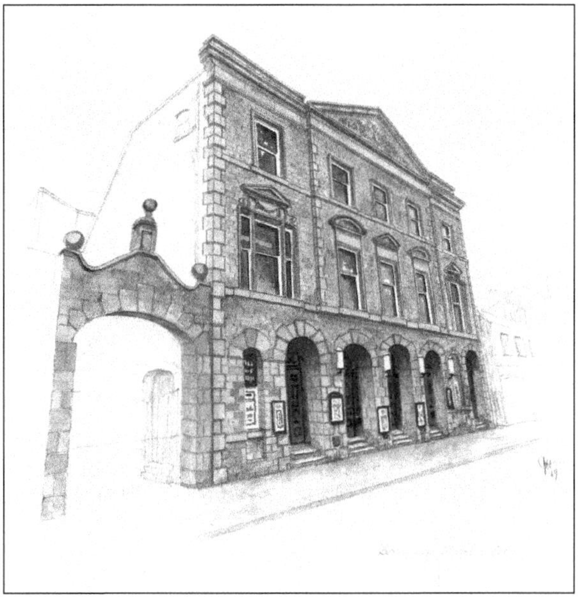

The Theatre Royal was a luxurious venue that hosted major stars of the day.

This gem of Victorian architecture was designed by renowned theatre designer Walter Emden, who was assisted by Herbert Crawshaw. Emden, whose credits included London's Garrick and Duke of York theatres, provided Barnsley with one of the finest classical style venues outside London.[27]

Built in 1898, the ground floor comprises a row of Gibbs surround arched entrance doors. Emden adds interest with alternating round and triangular pedimented first-floor windows. The three central ranges are set slightly forward between stone quoins. The deep cornice with a plain soffit and no decoration emphasises the crowning central pediment, which has an intricately decorated tympanum and a cartouche bearing the words 'Theatre Royal'.

The wide proscenium arch stage was 50 feet deep and cast-iron columns supported two horseshoe galleries with private boxes. The auditorium had gas lighting, American walnut and brass fittings and a domed ceiling had richly modelled baroque plasterwork by Jonas Bins & Son of Halifax. Unfortunately, in 1942 a fire caused significant damage to this plasterwork and the stage. Other alterations were made when Warner Brothers used the theatre for the Carl Reiner film *Bert Rigby, You're a fool* (1989).[28]

Barnsley has a long tradition of amateur theatre and music societies, which were an important part of the history of the Theatre Royal and Barnsley's other live entertainment venues. The St Cecilia Society gave their inaugural concert on 27 January 1875. The *Barnsley Chronicle* wrote: 'There have been many musical societies formed in the town but none gives greater promise of ultimate distinction than the St Cecilia Society.'

The Theatre Royal closed in 1957, reopened as a bingo hall in 1961, but was then left vacant for many years. The Friends of the Theatre Royal Trust, supported by Barnsley actor Brian Glover among others, campaigned to reopen the venue

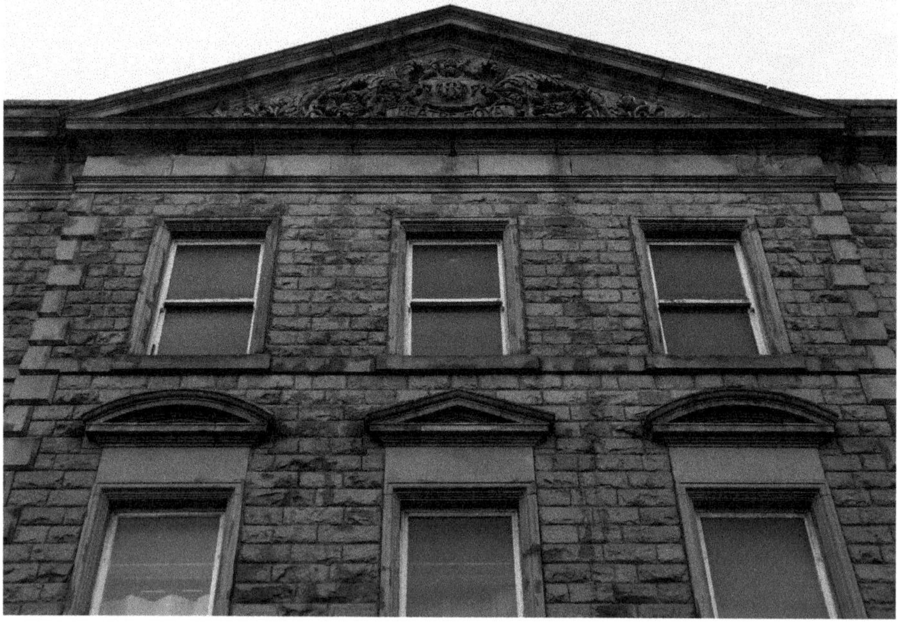

In 1907, it briefly became the Royal Opera House.

in the 1990s. While this ultimately failed, the money raised was used to open the Lamproom. The building was refurbished in 1995 and became a live music venue before reverting to a nightclub. The latest twist is the council bestowing a licence for the building to become a lap dancing club.[29]

38. National Westminster Bank

Before the Sheffield Banking Company opened this splendid-looking bank in 1913, the King's Head coaching inn occupied this site. In 1796, Barnsley's first private bank – Beckett, Birk's and Co. – was established by Joseph Beckett, brother of linen industry pioneer John Beckett. The Yorkshire Penny Bank, established by Colonel Edward Ackroyd in 1859, was the most prominent private bank in the town. Their free classical-style bank was built in 1903 at the corner of Market Hill and Eldon Street.

The even more impressively stylish building that replaced the King's Head was not built as a private bank. In 1916, Robert Eadon Reader wrote a book about the Sheffield Banking Company in which he claims that the formation of this bank, owned by shareholders in 1831, signalled the end of private banking. In 1919, the Sheffield Banking Company Ltd amalgamated with the National Provincial and Union Bank of England Ltd. This merged with the National Westminster Bank in 1969.[30]

Its heavily stylised façade makes this one of the finest-looking buildings in Barnsley, although it is not actually listed. However, the detailing on this ashlar

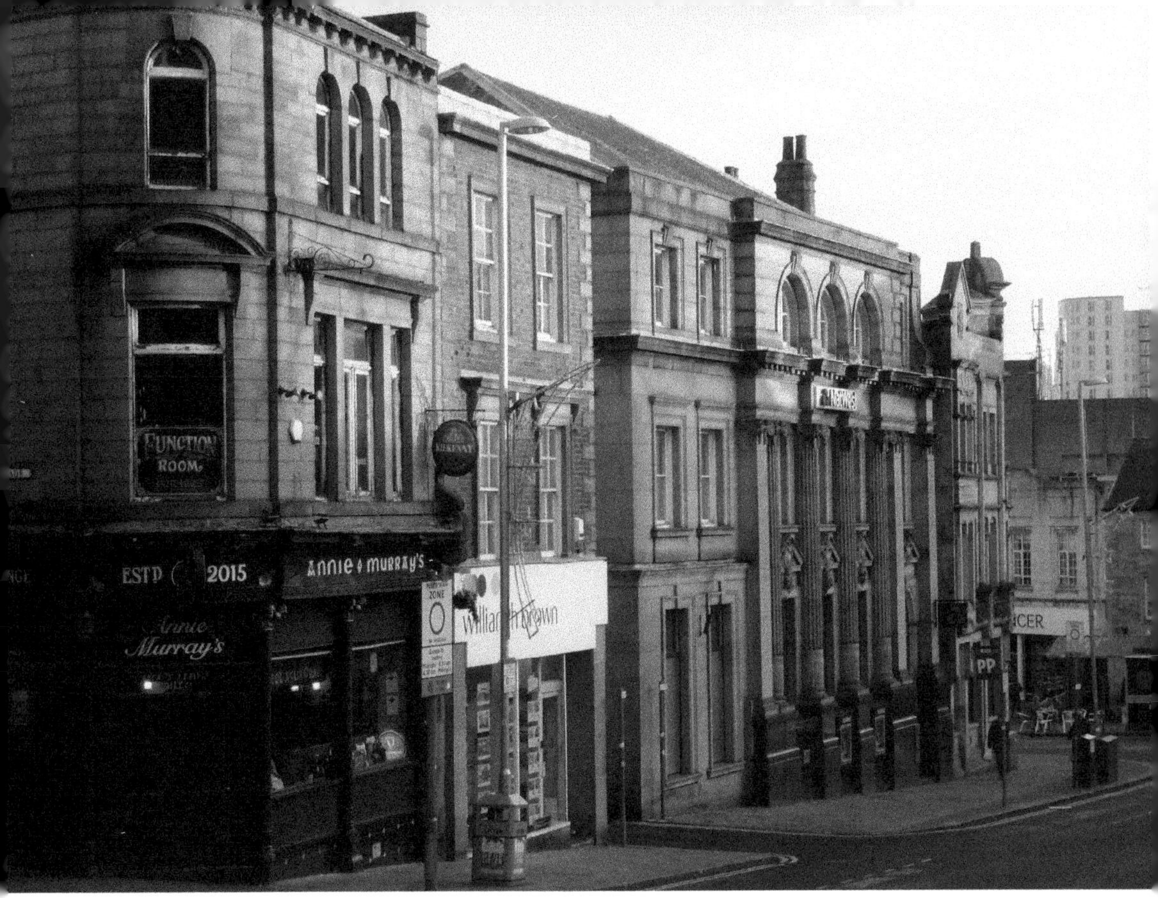

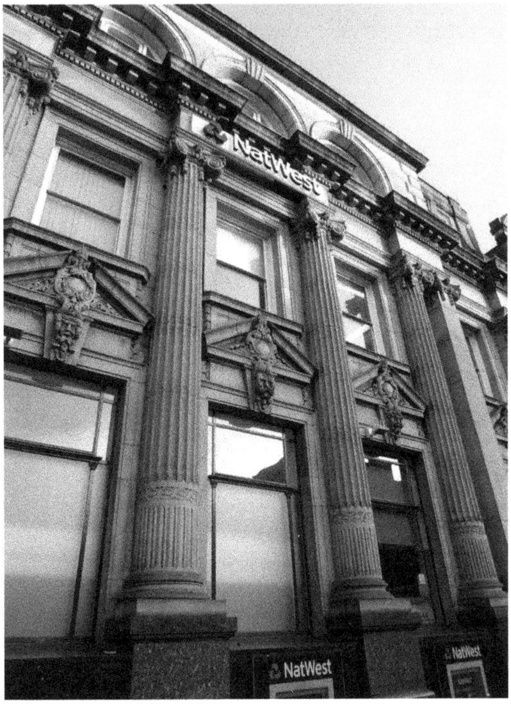

Above: The bank forms part of an uninterrupted classical façade along Market Hill.

Right: Keystones contain carved heads enclosed by serpents.

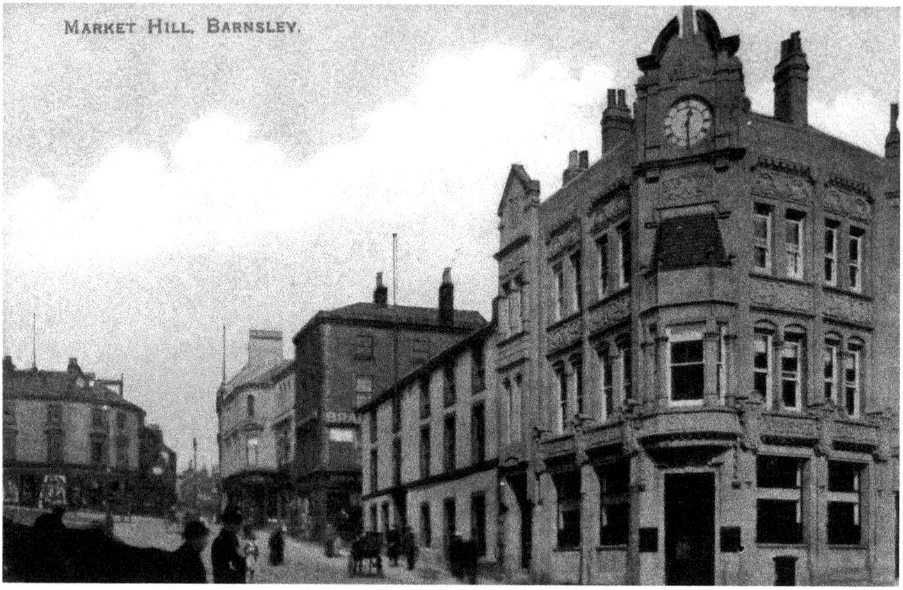

This image from 1910 shows the Kings Head Coaching Inn, built in around 1775.

stone post-Edwardian building shows just how prestigious the premises were. The dominant features are four fluted Ionic columns set on a tall, granite pedestal. These have diagonal volute Ionic capitals supporting a plain entablature with a weighty projecting cornice. Each of the central ground-floor windows has a pediment with a broken apex. Within the decorated tympanum is a cartouche connected to a supporting console containing sculptured faces.

On the upper level are three Diocletian windows, a classical motif derived from the Baths of Diocletian in Rome. The triumphal arch entrance set between pilasters is another classical device used on many early twentieth-century banks in order to make customers feel that their money is going to be well looked after.

The grand Victorian and Edwardian banks that were a feature of every high street are now in danger of extinction as on-line banking takes over. For security reasons there is only limited public access, but some decorative cornices and the grand staircase are visible to customers. Appropriate new uses can open up the original internal features to wider public enjoyment.

39. Former Barnsley Girls High School

The former Barnsley Girls High School is surrounded by a boundary wall and behind a wide grass verge opposite the Emmanuel Church, where the Old White Bear steps associated with John Wesley are now located.

The classical-style school building was designed by Arts and Crafts architects Buckland & Haywood-Farmer of Birmingham.[31] The Arts and Craft movement

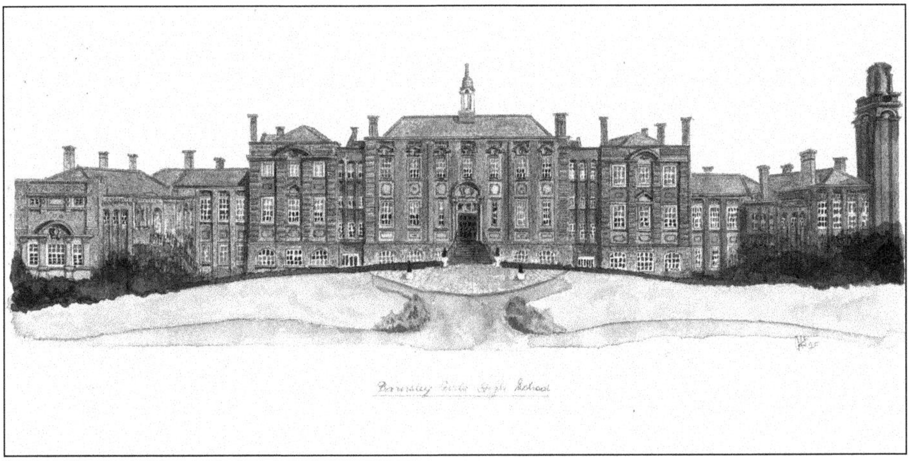

St Paul's in Hammersmith is another girls' school built at the turn of the century with Gustav Holst links – also red brick and stone.

was inspired by the writings of John Ruskin. Herbert Tudor Buckland was a leading exponent of the style, which placed particular emphasis on the intrinsic beauty of building materials. One of his finest works was the Royal Hospital School, built next to the River Stour in Suffolk in 1933.

The school, which was built in two phases, uses red Flemish-bond brickwork and ashlar stone. The original part, dating from 1905, is a central seven-bay block linked by three recessed narrow bays to three-bay blocks on each side. There are some strong references to classical motifs. The entrance is a reworked Palladian arch and the north wing contains a more unambiguous version of this

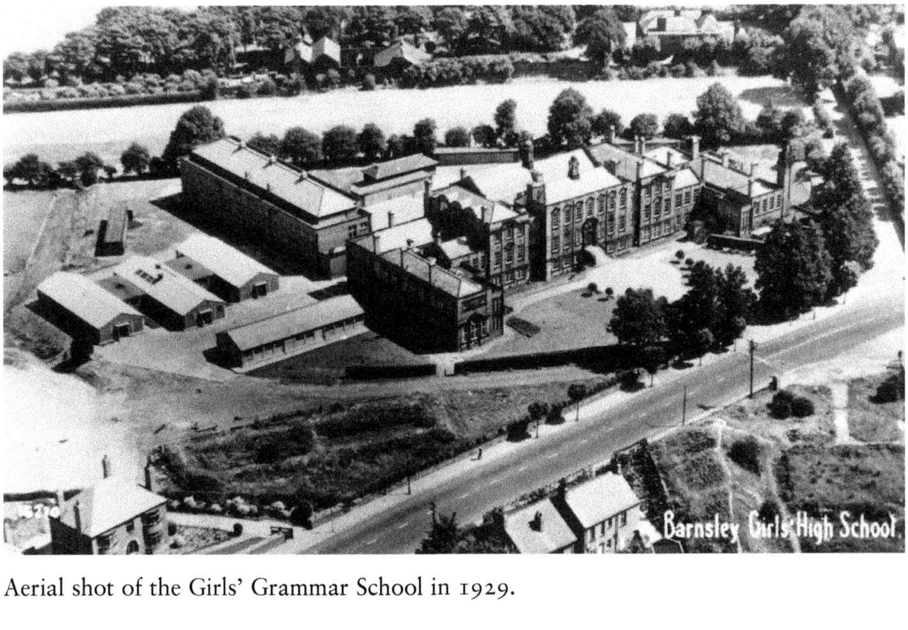

Aerial shot of the Girls' Grammar School in 1929.

detail. The use of Darley Dale stone dressings and moulded- and cut-brick details delivers a more attractive palette compared to sandstone buildings of the same period found in the town centre.

The school opened in November 1909, when the two-storey side elements to the left and right were added. The building has a central wooden lantern or cupola with round-arched openings and domed roof. On the central section there are open triangular pediments with a chessboard pattern over the upper twelve-pane sashes, which are set in architraves.

A flight of steps with iron railings leads up to the implied Palladian arch entrance, delineated by Ionic columns with a projecting curved segmented pediment enclosing a shield. The narrower windows on either side form the remainder of the arch. The entrance hall gave access to accommodation for over 400 girls and a nursery. The high level of teaching on offer is typified by the music teacher Alexander Hargreaves Ashworth having been a pupil of Gustav Holst.[32]

During the First World War the school grounds were used for food production and in the Second World War air-raid shelters were built near the playground. In the 1980s the school was acquired by Barnsley College and became the sixth form college. However, in 2000 the college sold it and the building was converted to private flats.

40. Barnsley Town Hall

For many decades the town's worthies had craved a more fitting Town Hall. The Old Town Hall, built in 1833 on St Mary's Gate, was described in the *Barnsley Chronicle* as being 'of dingy appearance' and 'out of keeping with a County Borough of Barnsley's size and importance'.

The new Town Hall was opened on 14 December 1933 by the immensely popular Prince of Wales, whose lunch included a Barnsley chop, chips and peas. The eponymous chop was invented by local butcher Albert Hirst. By December 1936 the charismatic prince had abdicated, making him far less popular. A slow-cooked double loin chop in rich gravy on the other hand is still enjoyed throughout the world.

Designed by Biggs and Thornley, the architects for Stormont in Belfast, the Town Hall is built of lustrous white Portland stone and has a very strict symmetrical design with a central tower. There is a rusticated ground floor below a band separating the two upper storeys. There is a clear hierarchy of windows with noticeably smaller upper-floor openings. Corinthian columns and pilasters adorn the ceremonial balcony.

To save money the original fussy tower was scrapped and a less pretentious one was reintroduced after construction had started. Nicholaus Pevsner was not overly impressed, describing the later addition as a 'bleak cubic' tower. However, the tower actually includes all the key elements of a classic steeple as described in

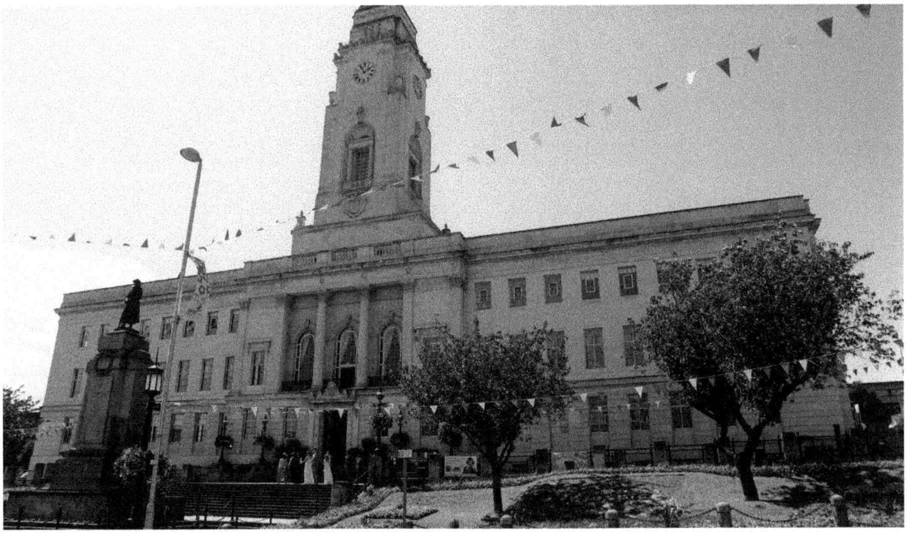

It would be hard to find a more prominent location for a Town Hall.

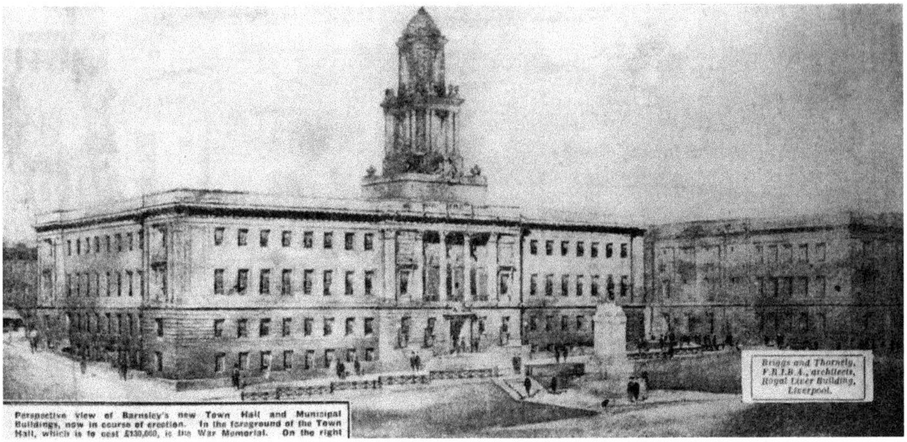

A 1931 planning drawing shows the ornate tower originally proposed.

James Gibbs' seminal *Book of Architecture* (1728). There is a clock on each face, openings similar to a belfry and a flagpole in the place of a weathervane. Recessed within each arched opening is a square arch with Roman lattice screen.

The profligate spending was criticised by George Orwell, who lived in Barnsley in 1936 while writing *The Road to Wigan Pier*. He thought it injudicious given the slum conditions of much of the housing in the vicinity.

Notwithstanding the criticism, the magnificent Town Hall is a centrepiece befitting of a town with such a proud heritage and in most people's opinion the tower is the crowning glory. The tower with a clock face on each side is by far the most distinguishing feature of the Barnsley skyline.

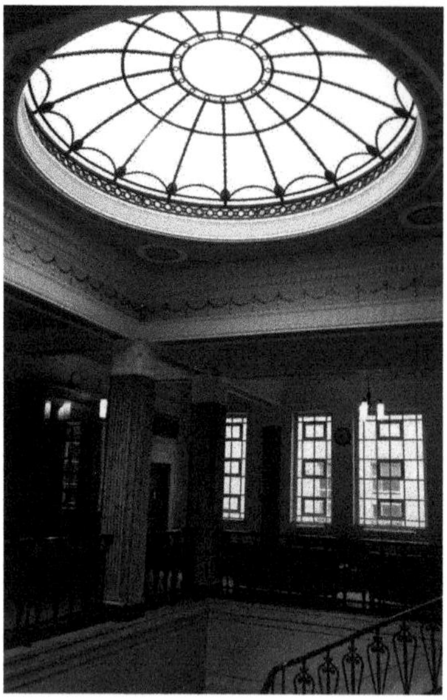

The central staircase, above which is a decorative ceiling with a superb skylight.

The Experience Barnsley Museum is a recent addition and there are many paintings and glass cabinets containing memorabilia, including one dedicated to Roy Mason, the former miner who became a cabinet minister.

41. The War Memorial and Barnsley Pals Centenary Square

The First World War memorial stands in front of the Town Hall. It predates the Town Hall and comprises a 2.4-metre sandstone pylon designed by architect William Thomas Curtis. On top of this pylon is a bronze statue by John Tweed. A soldier dressed in a greatcoat and a steel helmet has his bayonet fixed and rifle butt grounded.

Erected in 1925, the war memorial commemorated all those servicemen and women from the town who had died during the First World War. The imposing pylon is decorated with a wreath and cross. On the rear is a bronze plaque with a winged female figure holding a staff and a shield.

Local men volunteered at the Drill Hall on Eastgate (1896), now occupied by the *Barnsley Chronicle*. Many recruits were miners given that they were naturally fit and endured poor working conditions. The Thirteenth and Fourteenth battalions of the York and Lancaster Regiment were known as the Barnsley Pals. On the first day of the Battle of the Somme (1 July 1916) the Pals suffered terrible losses, with over 500 killed, missing and wounded.

The Town Hall was built as a purely civic building and to facilitate greater public use major changes were needed. It now houses the Experience Barnsley Museum, the archive, a café and a shop. Previously, the setting of the Town Hall was dominated by a grim sloping parking area, but this has been transformed

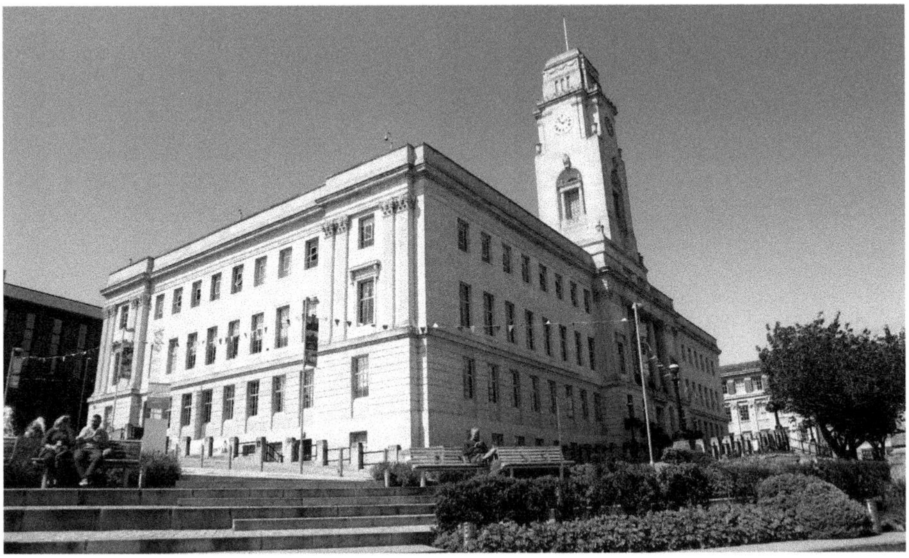

An attractive and well-used public space has been created.

with £2 million spent to create the Barnsley Pals Centenary Square. The square has a series of terraces in oatmeal granite with black granite banding to represent outcrops of coal. *Crossing Vertical*, a 10-metre-high oxidised Nigel Hall sculpture, sits on an ashlar stone plinth on the corner of Market Street. Stone steps lead to a water feature, a popular addition for children to enjoy on hot summer days. However, at night is when it comes to life. Thirty illuminated intermittent arching water jets are propelled by an underground plant room and 50,000-litre tank.

42. Mining and Technical College

The Mining and Technical College, which lies between the Town Hall and St Mary's Church, replaced and expanded the courses offered by the Harvey Institute on Eldon Street. The *Barnsley Chronicle* headline at that time claimed it was the largest mining college in the country. The technical college is separated from the Town Hall by Sadler Gate, named after the family of Sir Michael Sadler, who spoke at the opening in 1932. A famous educationalist and art collector, he was a benefactor who gave works of art to the Cooper Gallery.

The building is red brick with large areas of Portland stone that include grand Corinthian-style pilasters supporting a decorative entablature. According to Pevsner this building is of a classical revival style. There are three equally impressive elevations, with gauged brick arches over the windows and finely detailed Portland stone scroll consoles giving an indication of the high quality of buildings being erected in Barnsley during the 1930s.

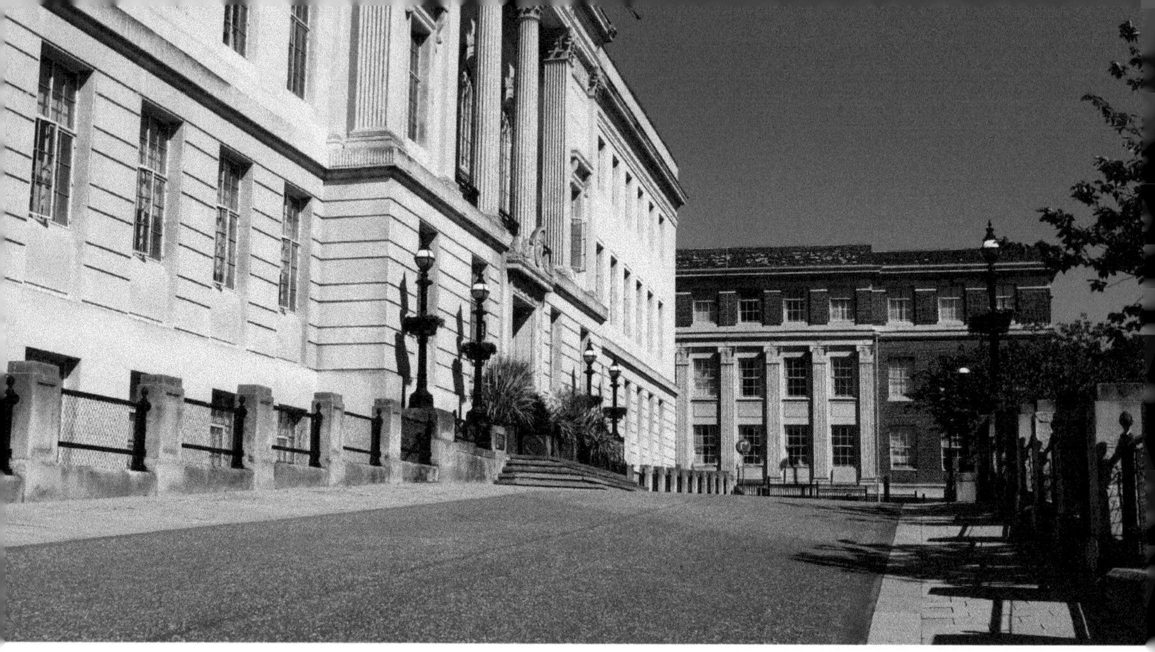

The college greatly enhances the setting of the Town Hall.

Old maps reveal the site previously contained an opulent residence called the Manor House. Behind this was the site of Barnsley's original workhouse. Barnsley opened its workhouse at St Mary's Place in around 1736. It is not surprising that the workhouse was opposite St Mary's Church as parish officials collected money to spend on poor relief for the sick.

There is some synergy in the mining college site having once contained a workhouse. Reliance on the workhouse was often caused by an industrial accident, which in Barnsley would be a constant fear given the poor health and safety record in the mining industry. Barnsley continued to run the old workhouse on St Mary's Place until a new union was formed on 15 January 1850 and the workhouse moved to a larger site on Gawber Road in 1852.

The Mining Technical College is now part of Huddersfield University, and a £5.5 million refurbishment has provided industry-standard TV and radio studios for journalism and media production students and sound-proof recording studios for music students. The prospectus also offers courses in hospitality management. This is all a far cry from the workhouse that once occupied the site, where hospitality was deliberately not on offer to discourage attendance.

43. Montague Burton Building

The white Portland stone Montague Burton building is meant to be highly prominent. Montague Burton employed estate agents Healey and Baker to find suitable sites in prominent locations, ideally occupying corners like this one at Barnsley. Built in 1930, it is positioned at the bottom of Market Hill across from Peel Square, on the corner of Queen Street and Eldon Street.

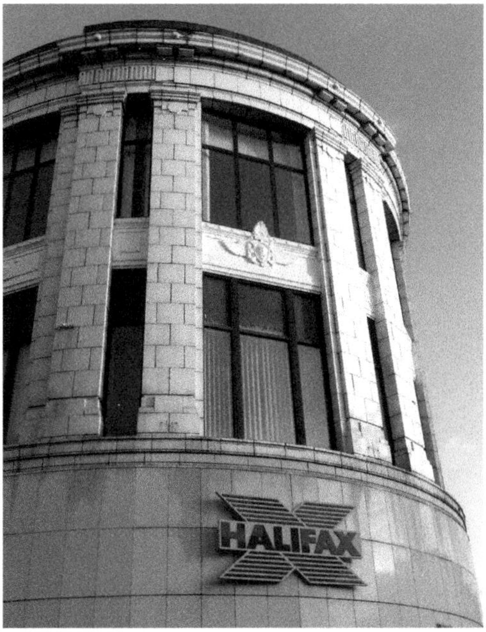

This prominent location is at the heart of the town centre.

Burton was the country's leading bespoke tailor, taking in-store measurements and sending these off to a factory in Leeds, employing around 10,000 staff. Between the wars many impressive Burton shops were built, often with upper-floor billiard halls that teetotal Montague Burton hoped would help prevent alcoholism in the young. There was already a billiard and snooker hall on Regent Street opposite the new courthouse. Therefore, this was the place to trip the light fantastic to 'Cherry Pink and Apple Blossom White' and other dance music made popular in the 1950s by the likes of Cuban-born bandleaders Perez Prado and Benny More. There was a Cuban ballroom here between 1948 and 1955.[33]

Many of the stores were bespoke like Burton suits, and often built of Portland stone. Harry Wilson was the company architect who developed Burton's trademark style. The new shops were described as 'modern temples of commerce'.[34] Harry Wilson was a fervent exponent of the art deco style, which often involved application of stylised geometric motifs. Architecture is an unavoidable public art form and Montague Burton buildings had a progressive influence on town centres.

Few shops were as distinct in their appearance as Montague Burton buildings, and they were viewed as beacons of modernity in their time. The modernist movement, which had its roots in the 1920s, considered that architecture had become stuck in the past. The machine age needed new architecture. Classical minimalism was one such reaction and classical influences can be seen in the Burton building. It has pilasters with a capital supporting all the elements of an entablature. There is a discernible cornice, frieze with embellishments, a taenia and architrave. The side entrance is below an octagonal window between decorated consoles.

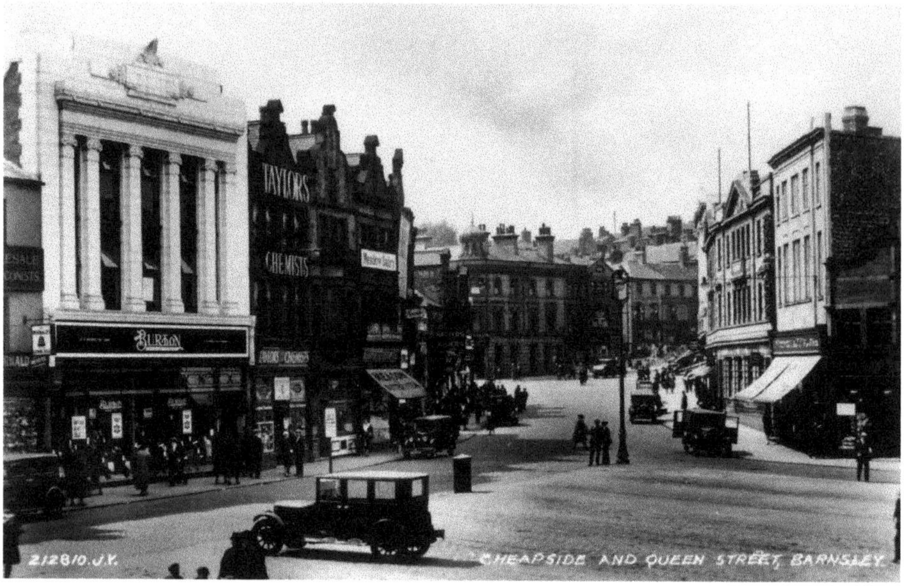

In 1935, the frontage along Queen Street included the Three Cranes Hotel.

44. Parkway Cinema

It was suggested to me recently that a whole book could be written about the lost cinemas of Barnsley. The list would include some highly impressive buildings – like the Palace, the Alhambra, the Pavilion and the Globe. Perhaps the glitziest of them all was the art deco-inspired, neon-lit façade of the Ritz on Peel Street. Barnsley's first purpose-built cinema, the Barnsley Electric Theatre, still stands on Eastgate, albeit no longer used as a cinema. However, the only remaining cinema currently in use is the Parkway Cinema on Eldon Street.

The highly ornate Empire Theatre, which was built in 1909, was converted to a cinema in 1920. It became the Gaumont before it was gutted by a fire on 2 January 1954. The Gaumont was rebuilt in 1956. The new modernist building was designed by T. P. Bennett & Sons and was renamed the Odeon in 1962. Sir Thomas Penberthy Bennett (1887–1980) ran one of the most successful architectural practices in the country.

Among their most notable buildings is the Saville Theatre on Shaftsbury Avenue. This building, which is decorated by a sculptural frieze, was later to become the Covent Garden Odeon. Bennett was also heavily involved in the development of post-war new towns, where the architecture followed principles set out by the pioneers of 1930s modernism such as Walter Gropius and Mies Van Der Rohe.

The Barnsley Odeon cinema closed down and the building lay dormant for almost two years before reopening as the Parkway Cinema in August 2007. Significant investment was made, but the 2020 pandemic has meant prolonged

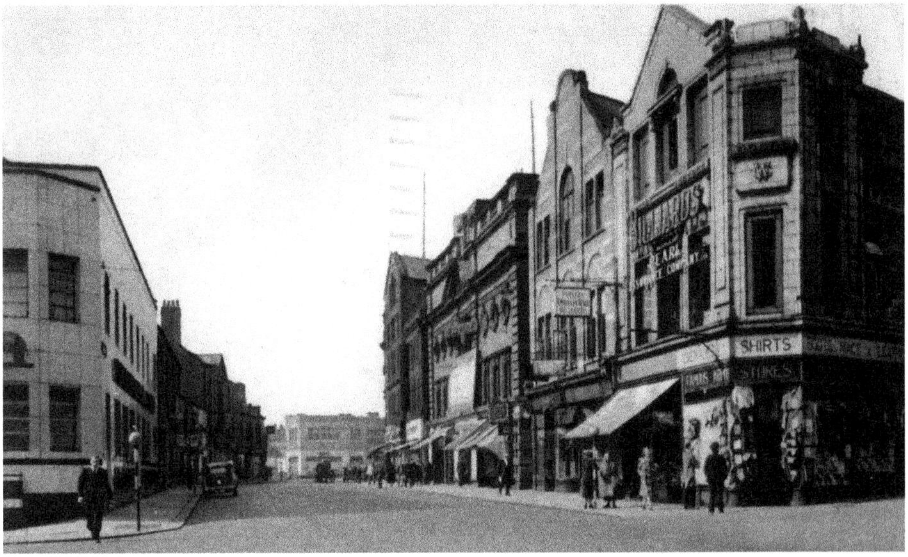

Eldon Street in 1935 shows the former Empire Cinema.

closure. In April 2021, the Cultural Recovery Fund allocated £72,763 to the Parkway to help reopening.[35]

Even after this investment challenges lie ahead. A new ten-screen multiplex cinema was due to be built above the Alhambra Centre. However, this was shelved after it was announced that a new thirteen-screen Cineworld would be included as part the council-backed Glassworks development.

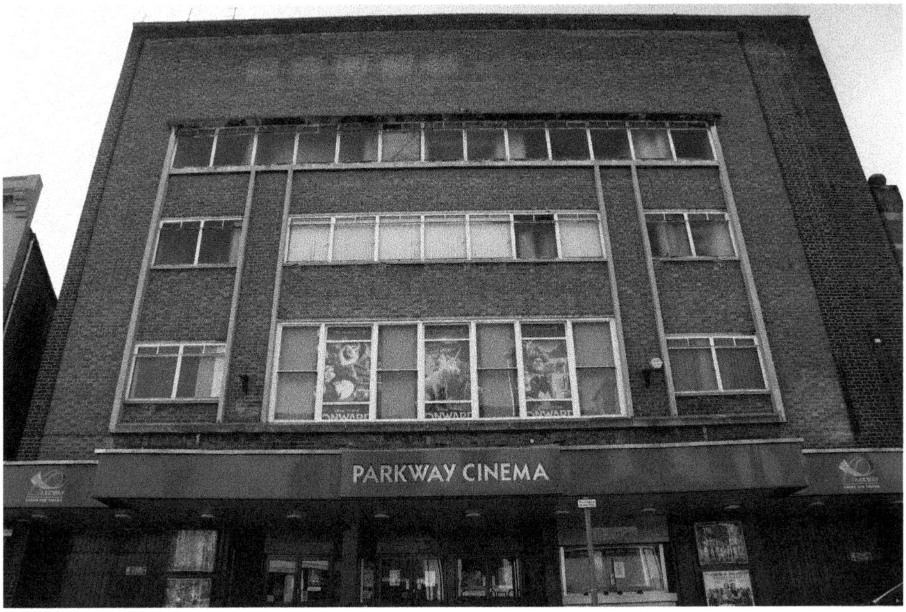

Modernist designs of this type were typical of post-war buildings.

Ever since the first purpose-built multiplex cinema opened in Milton Keynes in 1985 they generally have not been the most attractive buildings. The emphasis has been placed on providing luxurious auditoriums and technological innovations to improve the viewing experience. The new cinema in the Glassworks follows this rule, being an unashamedly no-frills structure that towers above most of its neighbours.

45. John Rideal House

This building from the late 1960s is synonymous with the post-war zeal of councils to rebuild. This was a very significant time for Barnsley's built heritage. There was a lot of demolition (and fire damage) that destroyed some highly significant and beautiful buildings, which, had they been retained, would undoubtedly have featured in this book. John Rideal House is included as a prime example of what was replacing the historic fabric in Barnsley's new Civic Quarter in the 1960s. It is also noteworthy for an unusual and controversial back story.

The building is named after a prominent local politician, who ironically tried very hard to conserve another of Barnsley's lost buildings, the Obelisk. John Rideal House was a Crown Building for use by the Department of Health and Social Security, so guaranteed many secure jobs.

John Rideal House occupies an elevated position on Barnsley's skyline.

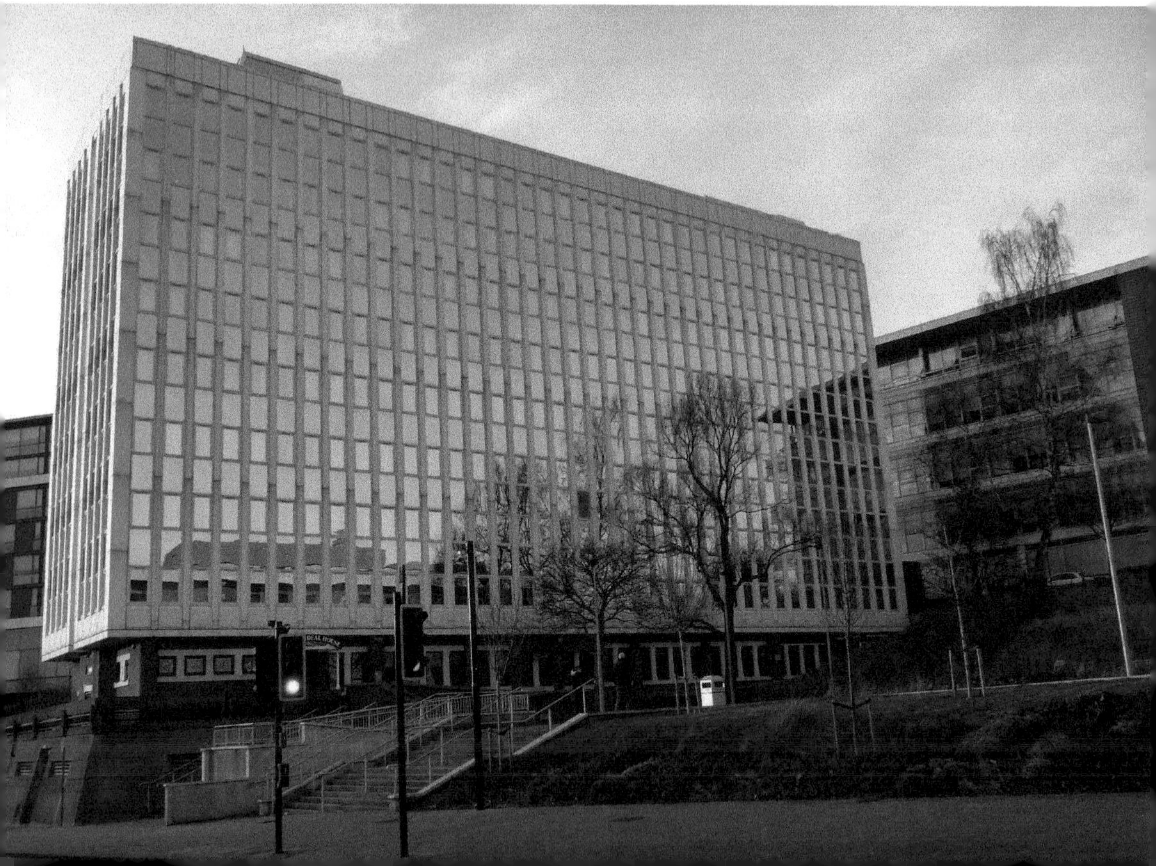

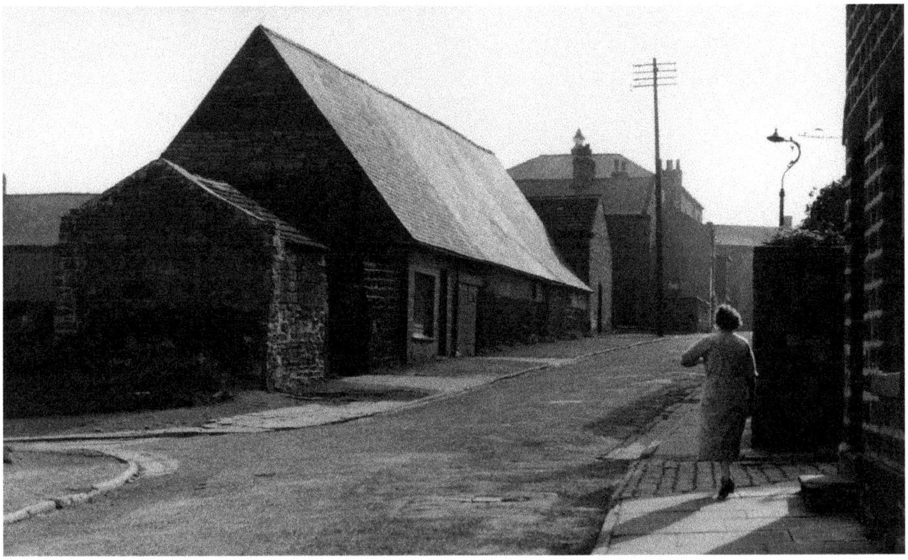

Westgate prior to demolition of the tithe barn in 1968.

There are few historic tithe barns left. While Gunthwaite Barn is located in the local area, Barnsley town centre had its very own tithe barn, which stood on Westgate for 500 years. Surely one of the town's most controversial decisions was to sanction the demolition of the tithe barn without legally securing its planned relocation.

In December 1967, the council allowed John Rideal House to be built and demolition of the historic barn subject to its relocation to another site. However, when this decision was made no immediate or firm plans existed concerning precisely where to rebuild the ancient timber barn. Reassurances were issued about safe storage and the Parks Department were to be responsible for this project in the vague hope it would eventually be relocated to Locke Park.[36]

While it was strongly asserted in official reports that great efforts were being made to store and accurately record all the timbers so the barn could be rebuilt, reports were emerging of stolen timbers as soon as November 1968. A revealing archaeological investigation into the restoration project was published in 1984. Virtually all of the timbers had disappeared and the only three remaining pieces of wood are now kept in storage at Canon Hall.[37]

46. Transport Interchange

The old bus station abutted railway arches associated with the former Court House station. These were all blocked up apart from one allowing access into the bus station. Despite the opportunity these provided for creating interesting shops and restaurants, the historic arches had already been demolished by the early 1970s. They were replaced by some short-lived, anonymous, single-storey shops that added nothing to the scene of Midland Street.

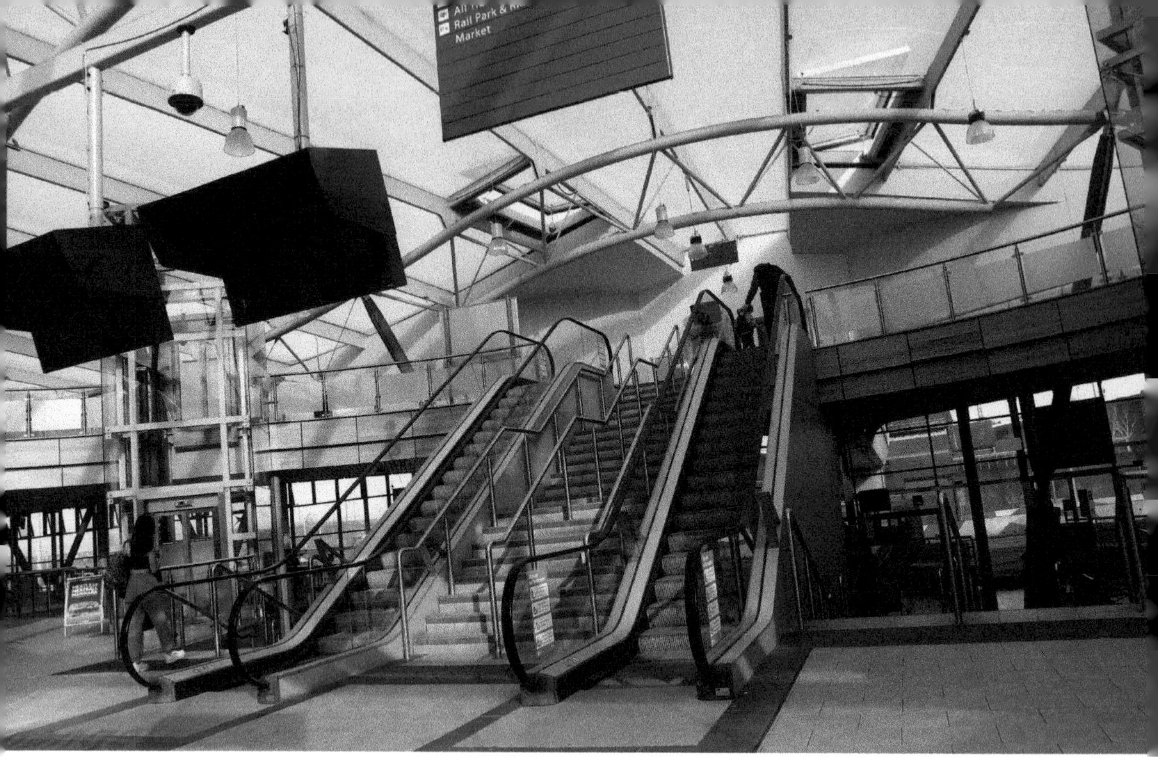

The interchange opened on 20 May 2007. Torrential rain caused it to close temporarily in August 2014.

The Interchange is a superb facility combining bus and train services that was designed by Sheffield-based architects Jefferson Sheard. It transformed this part of the town, which at one point had contained the cattle market. In 2003, the council chose Stirling Prize winner Will Alsop to head Remaking Barnsley. Alsop's vision was to create a modern version of a Tuscan wall by having a circle of iconic new buildings surrounding Barnsley's Town Hall. His vision also included beaming a halo of light hundreds of feet into the air to capture Barnsley in a golden glow. The Interchange was the first Remaking Barnsley project to be completed and the striking design fits perfectly with Alsop's vision.

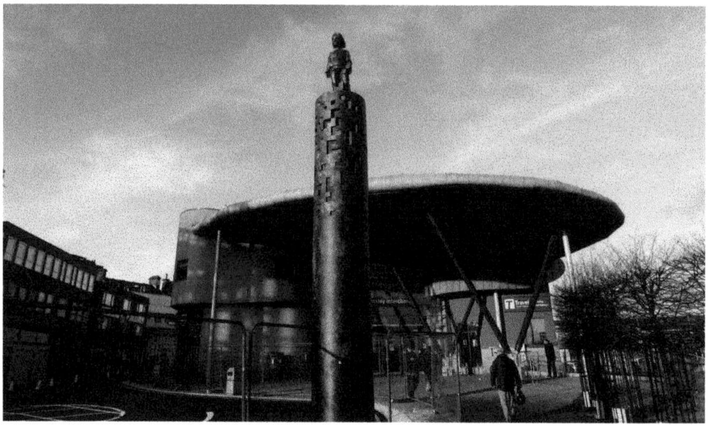

This fine sculpture was erected in Interchange Square in April 2012.

The railway station on Schwabisch Gmund Way is named after Barnsley's twin town in Barden-Wurttemberg. Barnsley also has the only road in the country called Tank Row.

When in 2017 Barnsley featured on the BBC 2 series *This Dancing Town* the dance sequences ended around a sculpture by Glasgow-based artist Kenny Hunter located at the Kendray Street entrance to the Interchange. The presenter, Steve Elias, expressed his admiration for the sculpture of a small child stood on the Barnsley bed seam of coal. The column reflects the importance of coal mining in Barnsley's past, but the child on top is symbolic of the town's future. There is black patina which it was envisaged would gradually wear away to reveal the bronze sculpture below.

47. Barry Hines House

In July 2019, the 50th anniversary of the film *Kes* based on the book *A Kestrel for a Knave* was celebrated with the installation of a blue plaque on author Barry Hines' former house. Barry, who was born on 30 June 1939 in Hoyland Common, died in 2016 after writing many notable books and screenplays. The Barnsley and England school footballer was a Physical Education teacher who went on to write for television and radio. His 1984 drama-documentary *Threads* was about the aftermath of a nuclear strike on Sheffield, where Hines worked in the university. Local author Milly Johnson, *Kes* director and producer Ken Loach and Tony Garnett were among those at the plaque unveiling.

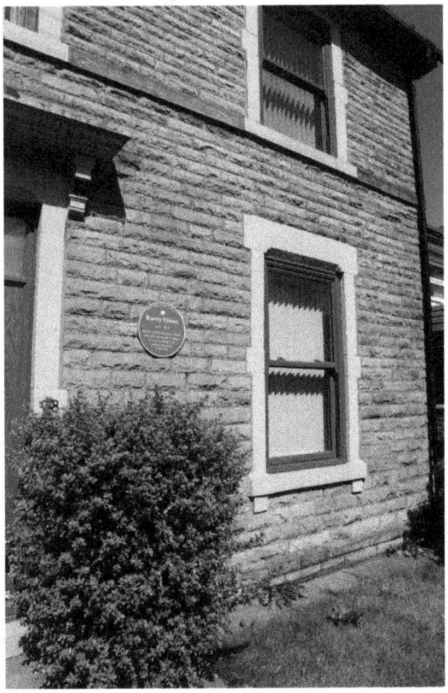

The Barry Hines blue plaque was sponsored by the Yorkshire Society.

In 1977, the two-part TV play *The Price of Coal* showcased upcoming northern comics including Barnsley-born Stan Richards, who became Seth Armstrong in *Emmerdale*. It initially shows preparations for a royal visit to Thorpe Hesley (a disused colliery in Rotherham) by Prince Charles. The second part deals with a mining disaster that takes place shortly after the royal visit.

A Kestrel for a Knave is about wasted potential caused by a failed education system that produced 'dead end' secondary moderns with cane-wielding headmasters. The kestrel that Billy Casper takes from a nest at a farm in Hoyland Common symbolises the escape from his situation. The book's preface explains that the title harks back to medieval times when only the aristocracy could own most hawks, while knaves could only own kestrels.

Kes launched the careers of hitherto unknowns from Barnsley Brian Glover, who played Mr Sugden, the sadistic PE teacher, and David Bradley (Billy Casper).

Though born in Sheffield, Brian Glover attended Barnsley Grammar School and was an English teacher in Barnsley. Following in his father's footsteps he was also a professional wrestler, going under the name Leon Arras the Man From Paris. Brian Glover got the part in *Kes* due to his being a close friend of Barry Hines, who was a teacher at Kirk Balk School in Hoyland.

48. Barnsley College

This imposing, unashamedly modern college is another Jefferson Sheard design. It was built in the age of austerity and the cladding materials were changed from those initially planned. A shimmering green duotone was replaced by bold red cladding, with green fins on the rear elevation to add contrast. The brash colour scheme on the rear section irritates some. However, the front of the building, which is designed to slope down to better reflect the scale of the adjacent conservation area, has a more restrained finish.

This building has an active frontage as there are public spaces that can be accessed without needing to use the main entrance. Courses on offer include catering and hair and beauty. The urban park at the rear is open to all and the building extends out over a generous public concourse with seating and ashlar stone totems. The college is fully integrated with the town centre and there is an easy synergy to the footways that pass the nearby Oaks Memorial, Dickie Bird statue and Peace Gardens.

The new building replaced a former college that was well liked. This was a unique building because of the lecture theatre on the roof. This space was used as a regular venue for concerts. John Lil, a Tchaikovsky Prize winner, played a piano recital on 12 October 1967 at which there was to be no smoking and no stilettos.

Further back in time the site contained a fine house and the Obelisk, a prominent local landmark, stood at the junction of Old Mill Lane and Church Lane and is one of Barnsley's many lost treasures. It was designed and built by local architect

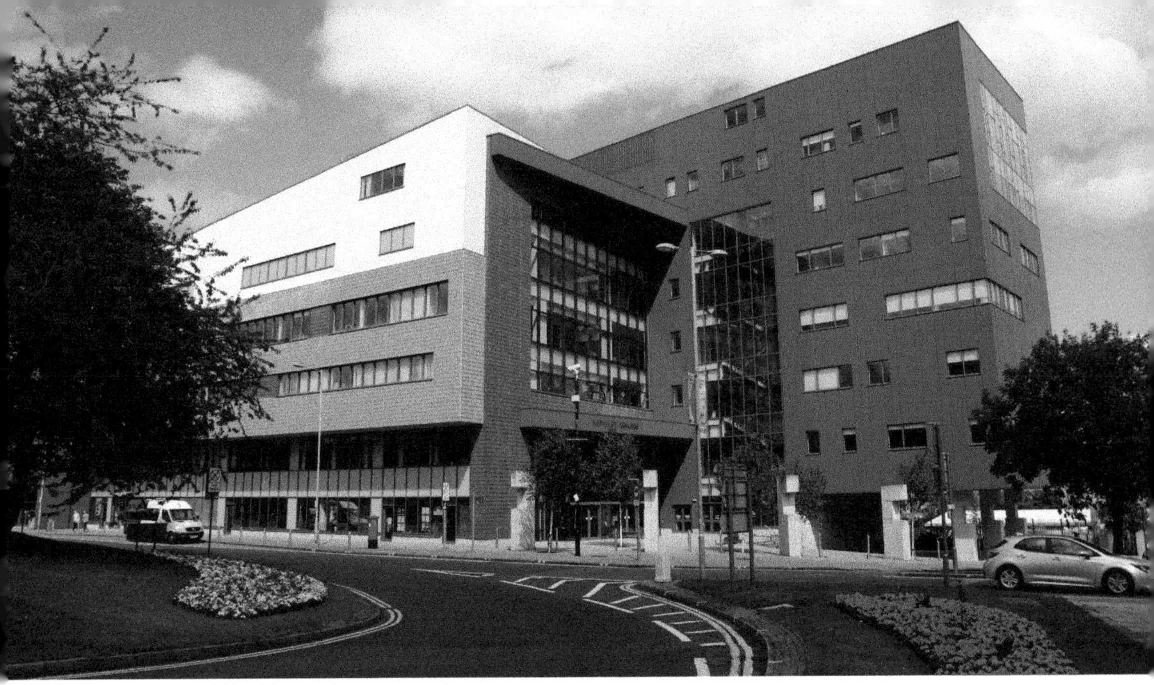

Behind the college is an urban park that is open to everyone.

John Whitworth and was also known as the Mence monument after the local family of parsons that served at St Mary's. Another alternative name was Peterloo Tower (after the massacre of the same year in 1819). The Obelisk was a grand gateway feature at a key route into the town.

In 1931, when the decision was made to demolish the Obelisk, Councillor Rideal voted against the decision as 'the whole town was against it' and the

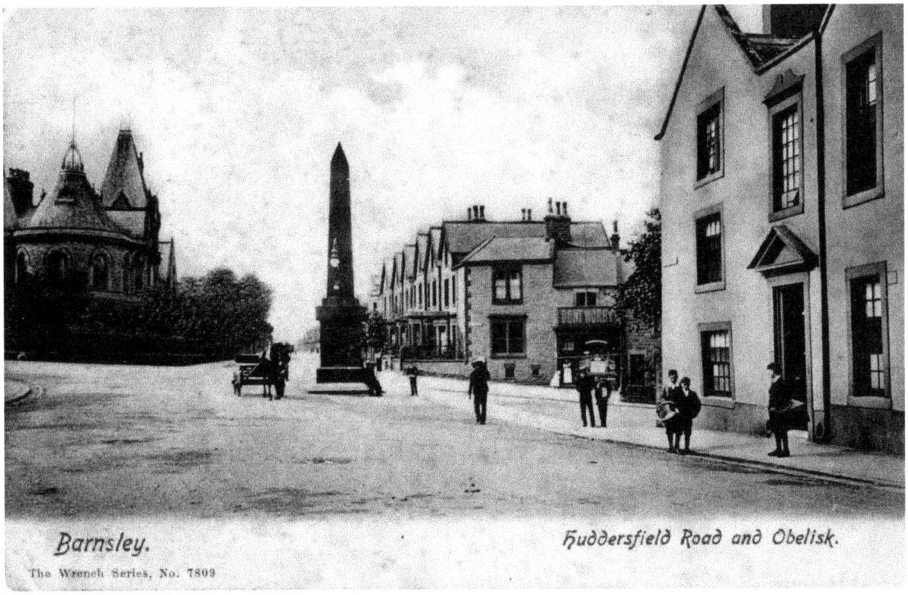

In 1903, the obelisk was next to a grand house that occupied the site of the college.

Barnsley Chronicle reported that a petition had been submitted against the loss of this relic. The rector of St Mary's Church wrote about the loss in the parish magazine, referring to high-handed action of the council.

49. Barnsley Sixth Form College

Barnsley Sixth Form College sits within a cluster of tall buildings on the highest point of the town centre. Will Alsop asserted that the hilly topography within Barnsley meant it had Tuscan qualities and a Building Heights Study was prepared to preserve the distinctive Barnsley skyline. A critical design consideration was ensuring that the new college did not challenge the dominance of the Town Hall, particularly when viewed from Church Street and Market Hill.

The college replaced the town's library and also removed twelve ugly, concrete, canopied commercial units and decked parking built in the 1970s. Having the main entrance on St Mary's Place was also important in order to connect with the Barnsley PALS Centenary Square. The fully glazed lobby maximises the transparency of the building and is angled to reflect an image of the Town Hall.

As well as matching the Town Hall with the use of dressed Portland stone cladding, the contrasting bronze/brass-coloured cladding makes the front elevation very attractive. However, I doubt if many would realise that this colour was specifically chosen to reflect the heritage of brass bands in the area.

The new sixth form college provides a superb backdrop to the Barnsley Pals Centenary Square.

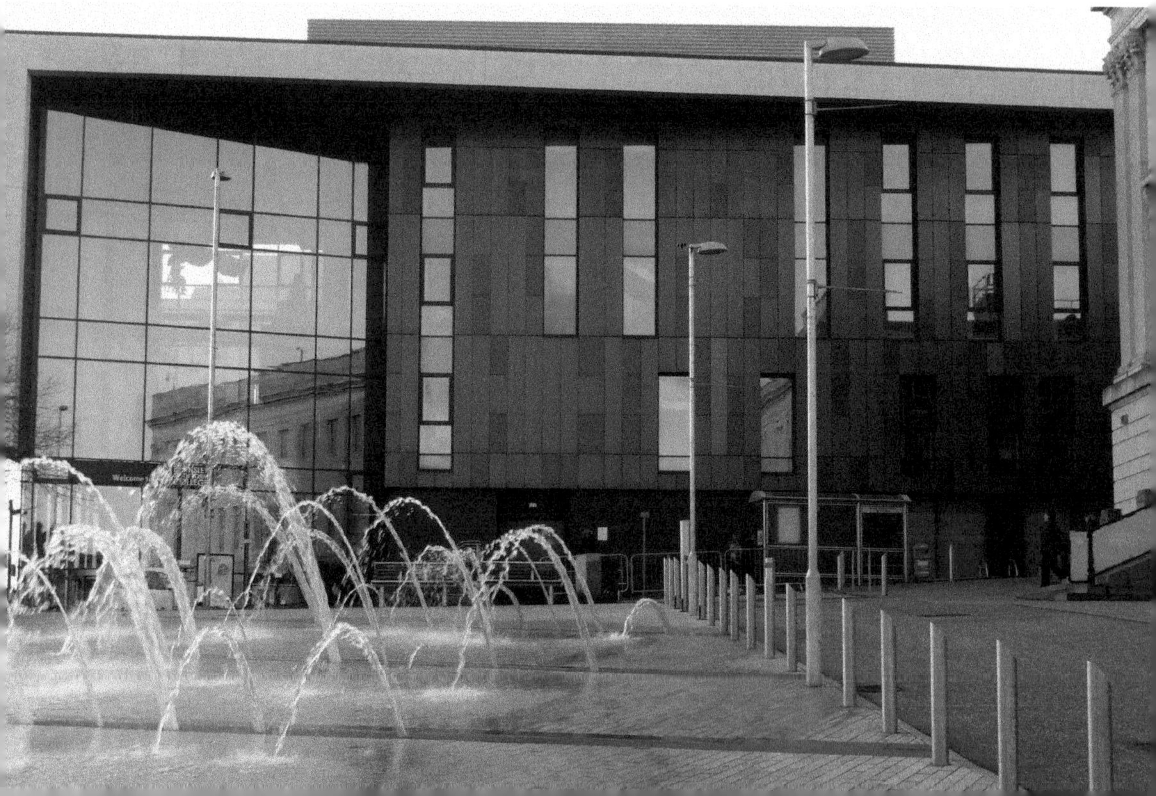

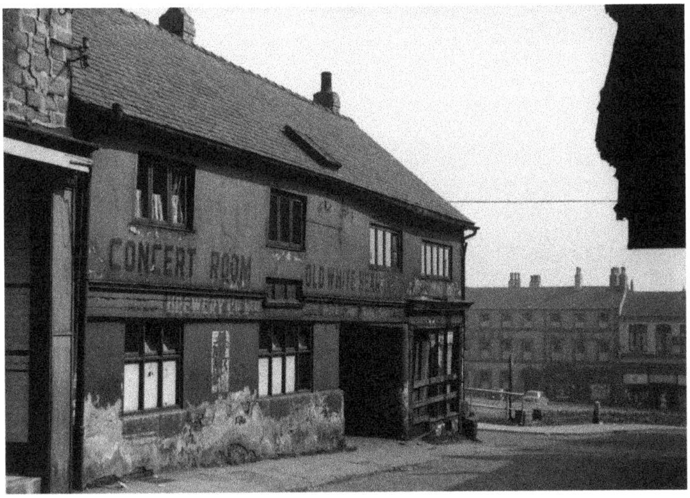

The Old White Bear in 1960. The South Yorkshire Miners' Association was formed here.

Long ago the site contained one of the town's most historically significant buildings, the Old White Bear public house. The earliest record of this building's existence is when it was the venue for a dinner during Barnsley Races in 1717.

In 1786, an aged John Wesley preached at the Old White Bear. The steps on which he stood are preserved outside the Emmanuel Church on Huddersfield Road. In 1798, Barnsley's first known professional theatrical production occurred when William Collier and William Huggins touring company appeared in the Old White Bear Yard.[38]

50. Lightbox and Glassworks

After being hit hard by austerity Barnsley Council decided to take the initiative to attract new businesses. The Glassworks comprises a new indoor market and shopping centre anchored by a multiscreen cinema and tenpin bowling. The name was chosen to evoke Barnsley's industrial heritage and it includes a new town centre library building called the Lightbox.

The Lightbox, which opened in the spring of 2019 is aptly named as the main design motif is utilisation of mirrored glass to reflect the surroundings. While effective in changing the reflected image from where you approach, Barnsley's pre-eminence in Glass manufacture could be more artistically honoured. Nevertheless, the building works internally and provides a first-class environment in which to browse the library books and sit and enjoy the other facilities on offer.

When Ian Nairn visited Barnsley in the 1970s there was still a generous open market on May Day Green. The trading area of the small medieval market had been extended in 1874 and on market days people flocked to May Day Green from miles around. Nairn's documentary shows fairground rides on one side and rows of market stalls, but he points out that there are no longer any historic buildings around May Day Green.

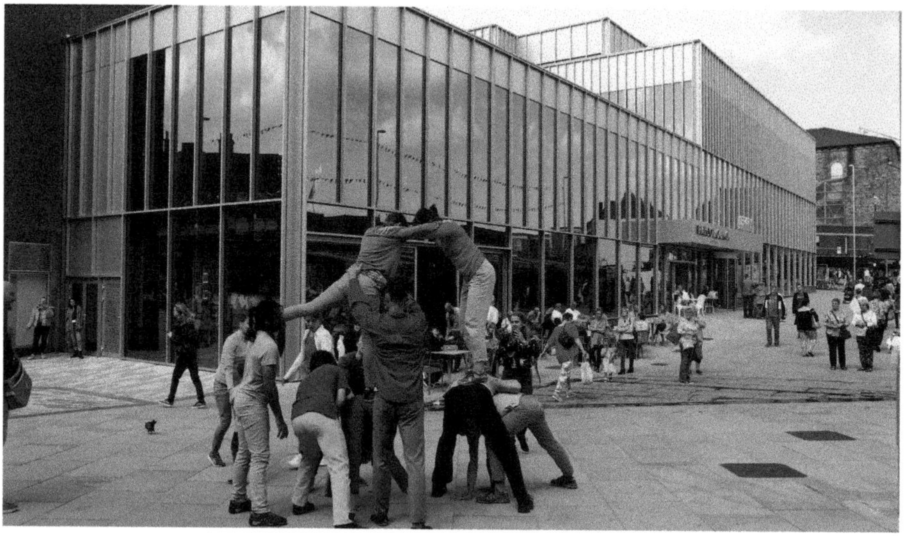

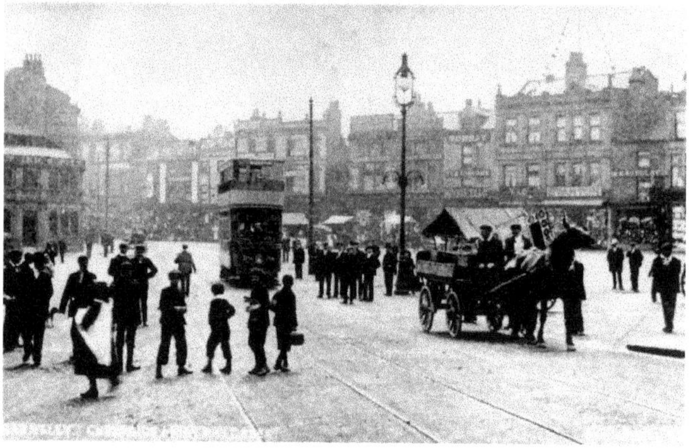

Above: Recreating a large public space provides an opportunity for vibrant street theatre.

Left: May Day Green in 1900 showing trams and horse-drawn carts.

Nairn, who has written about place and locality being swept away by post-war town planners, was unimpressed with plans for the new Metropolitan Centre.[39] Brutalism is a form of modernism that derives from the French *beton brut*, meaning raw concrete. Many brutalist buildings are composed of visually stimulating geometric forms. The Magistrates' Court on Westgate works well. The Metropolitan Centre, on the other hand, was a dispiritingly grey place with a small outdoor market.

It is hoped that the Glassworks will have the same visitor attraction that extending the market had in 1847. An enlarged public space has been designed to reflect the craggy nature of the Pennine Hills and accommodate the Sough Dyke that still exists below ground. Graham Ibbotson has produced another iconic sculpture as a centrepiece for the new open space. This is claimed to be the first public artwork to commemorate the victims of Covid-19 and celebrate key workers. The artwork includes a poem by the Bard of Barnsley, Ian McMillan.

Notes

1. Curtis, A., 'Mill of the Black Monks; Recording of Historic Graffiti' (ArcHeritage unpublished reports, ads Archaeology DataService, 2019).
2. historyofparliamentonline.org, The Institute of Historic Research.
3. Mel Dyke, *All for Barnsley Celebrities Remember the Town* (Wharncliffe Publishing Ltd, 2003).
4. 'Papers of the Bosville-MacDonald Family of Gunthwaite, Thorpe and Skye', Hull History Centre.
5. *Cannon Hall Museum Park and Gardens: The Guidebook*, www.ledgardjepson.com.
6. vam.ac.uk.
7. 'Memories of Barnsley' in association with the *Barnsley Chronicle*, Issue 8, Winter 2008.
8. 'Memories of Barnsley' in association with *Barnsley Chronicle*, Issue 37, Spring 2006.
9. taskertrust.co.uk.
10. Alliott, Gerald J., *The Vanishing Relics of Barnsley* (Wharncliffe Publishing Ltd, 1996).
11. 'Memories of Barnsley' in association with the *Barnsley Chronicle*, Issue 8, Winter 2008.
12. victoriaonlinesightseeing.com.
13. changingvancouver.wordpress.com.
14. 'Memories of Barnsley' in association with *Barnsley Chronicle*, Issue 22, Summer 2012.
15. 'Memories of Barnsley' in association with *Barnsley Chronicle*, Issue 17, Spring 2011.
16. Webster, N. W., *Joseph Locke Railway Revolutionary* (George Allen and Unwin, 1970).
17. Hoskins, W. G., *The Making of the English Landscape* (Pelican Books, 1955).
18. Webster, N. W., *Joseph Locke Railway Revolutionary* (George Allen and Unwin, 1970).
19. 'The Carlile Institute, Meltham', Huddersfield Exposed.
20. 'Memories of Barnsley' in association with *Barnsley Chronicle*, Issue 17, Spring 2011.
21. Jessop, Eric Longford, *Barnsley Brass* (Wharncliffe Books, 2006).

22. Darlow, Paul, *The Oakes Disaster 1866: A Living History* (Heritage Lottery Fund).
23. 'Memories of Barnsley' in association with the *Barnsley Chronicle*, Issue 17, Spring 2011.
24. *Ibid.*
25. Dyke, Mel, *All for Barnsley Celebrities Remember the Town* (Wharncliffe Publishing Ltd, 2003).
26. *Rothmans Football Yearbook 1971–72* (The Queen Anne Press Ltd).
27. theatrestrust.org.uk.
28. *Ibid.*
29. examinerlive.co.uk, 10 September 2020.
30. natwestgroup.com/heritage.
31. 'Memories of Barnsley' in association with *Barnsley Chronicle*, Issue 29, Spring 2014.
32. 'Memories of Barnsley' in association with *Barnsley Chronicle*, Issue 31, Autumn 2014.
33. taskertrust.co.uk.
34. buildingourpast.com.
35. ITV News, 2 April 2021.
36. Alliott, Gerald J., *The Vanishing Relics of Barnsley* (Wharncliffe Publishing Ltd, 1996).
37. *Ibid.*
38. 'The History of Theatres in Barnsley', *Around Town Magazine* (8 November 2017).
39. Nairn, Ian, *Nairn's Towns* (Notting Hill Editions Ltd, 1967).

Bibliography

Alliott, Gerald J., *The Vanishing Relics of Barnsley* (Wharncliffe Publishing Ltd, 1996)

Aspects of Barnsley, Volumes 1–7 (Wharncliffe Books, 1996)

Bailey, Catherine, *Black Diamonds* (Penguin Books, 2007)

Cannon Hall Museum Park and Gardens: The Guidebook, ledgardjepson.com

Clarke, Basil F. L., *Church Builders of the Nineteenth Century* (David and Charles Reprints, 1969)

Curtis, A., 'Mill of the Black Monks; Recording of Historic Graffiti' (ArcHeritage unpublished reports, ADS Archaeology DataService, 2019)

Darlow, Paul, *The Oakes Disaster 1866: A Living History* (Heritage Lottery Fund, 2017)

Dyke, Mel, *All for Barnsley: Celebrities Remember the Town* (Wharncliffe Publishing Ltd, 2003)

Elliott, Brian, *Pitts and Pitmen of Barnsley* (Wharncliffe Books, 2001)

Elliott, Brian, *Barnsley History from the Air: 1926–1939* (Wharncliffe Publishing Ltd, 1994)

Elliott, Brian, *Barnsley: 1890s–1990s* (Sutton Publishing Ltd, 1999)

Fleming, John, Hugh Honour and Nickolas Pevsner, *Dictionary of Architecture* (Pelican Books, 1980)

Hill, Christopher, *Reformation to Industrial Revolution*, Volume 2 (Pelican Books, 1969)

Hoskins, W. G., *The Making of the English Landscape* (Penguin Books, 1955)

'Huddersfield Exposed', The Carlile Institute, Meltham

Lewis, Michael J., *The Gothic Revival* (Thames & Hudson, 2002)

Lockhart, Ben et al, 'The Glassworks of the Rylands Family and Hiram Codd', sha.org.

Longford Jessop, Eric, *Barnsley Brass* (Wharncliffe Books, 2006)

'Memories of Barnsley', *Barnsley Chronicle*, various editions

Nairn, Ian, *Nairn's Towns* (Notting Hill Editions Ltd, 1967)

'Papers of the Bosville-MacDonald Family of Gunthwaite, Thorpe and Skye', Hull History Centre.

penninewaterways.co.uk/barnsley

Pevsner, Nikolas, *Pioneers of Modern Design* (Pelican Books, 1936)

Pevsner, Nikolas, *The Buildings of England – Yorkshire: The West Riding* (Penguin Books, 1959)

Rothmans Football Yearbook: 1971–72 (The Queen Anne Press Limited)
Stevens Curl, James, *Victorian Churches* (BT Batsford Ltd/English Heritage, 1995)
Tasker, E. G., *Barnsley Street*, Volumes 1–5 (Wharncliffe Books, 2003)
theatrestrust.org.uk
Webster, N. W., *Joseph Locke Railway Revolutionary* (George Allen and Unwin, 1970)

Acknowledgements

I would like to thank the following: the owners and occupiers of the fifty buildings featured in this book, especially the rector, churchwardens and PCC of St Mary's Church, Barnsley, for kindly allowing me to photograph the church; Jenny Griffiths for allowing me on to her working farm; Eviee Bowden, Front of House Supervisor at the Civic; Mark Simpson and Babeth Bettencourt at the Transport Interchange and SYPTE; all the staff of the Barnsley Archive, led by Paul Stebbing; architect Mark Booth for suggestions for buildings to include and local knowledge; members of the Barnsley Civic Choir, including John Higgins, Sue Rose and Derek Hollingsworth; Alan Parks and the Barnsley Civic Trust; the Tasker Trust for their comprehensive collection of archive material; Paul Darlow at the NUM archive; council officers including Nick King, Tony Wiles, Lynn Dunning, Nicola Grierson and Jo Birch have all helped with background information and kindly answered my questions; Kevin Liddy and Nathan Cantrell provided some excellent information; Megan Evans and all at National Trust Images for their kind consideration in allowing the use of the Wentworth Castle photographs; and Stewart and Duncan at Marshalls Direct for the map.

In cases where good photographs were hindered by street furniture, boundary walls or other factors, John Higgins' illustrations are perfect. I would not have embarked on this journey at all without the encouragement of Christopher Marsden on my first day of retirement. Finally, I would like to thank my partner, Sandra Haigh, and our friend June Jowett-Durkin for proofreading.

About the Author and Illustrator

After his parents moved south from Liverpool, Kentish man Keiron grew up by the seaside. He studied town planning in Leeds and now resides in the shadow of the Pennine Hills. Working across many planning disciplines, most enjoyment came from project managing public art and environmental improvements and travelling around Ireland as a planning inspector. A parish councillor for sixteen years, he learnt bell-ringing and is a member of the Mirfield Choral Society and Barnsley Civic Choir. A season ticket holder with his son at Goodison Park, he has visited many football grounds – from Fratton to Celtic Park. Eclectic in his listening habits, he has visited many great theatres and concert halls.

John is a published author of theatrical books, which include *Theatres of Achievement* and *West End in Watercolour: A Portrait of London Theatre*. His expertise in the theatre comes via the orchestra pit after many years as a musical director, notably playing Sheffield's Lyceum Theatre and City Hall among other venues. He has also written two full-scale musicals. As choirmaster for the Barnsley Civic Choir, he has conducted the town's annual carol service for around thirty years and regularly plays the organ at Barnsley's Emmanuel Methodist Church.